The
Poetry of
Charles
Baudelaire

The Poetry of Charles Baudelaire

This edition published in 2019 by Arcturus Publishing Limited
26/27 Bickels Yard, 151–153 Bermondsey Street,
London SE1 3HA

AD006519UK

Printed in the UK

Contents

Poems in Prose

Introduction

Charles Baudelaire was born on 9 April 1821 in Paris. He was the son of François Baudelaire and his young wife Caroline Defayis. Baudelaire's father died in 1827, and he and his mother spent the next year and a half in bliss together before Caroline remarried in November of 1828. Her new husband, Jacques Aupick, was a career soldier. In 1831, he was transferred to Lyons. Baudelaire attended the Collège Royal in Lyons before returning to Paris and starting at the Lycée Louis-le-Grand in 1836. His teachers were impressed by his poetry, but his attitude and behaviour concerned them. He tended to act older than his age and withdraw into himself.

After his expulsion in 1839, he pretended to be a law student at the École de Droit while living freely in the Latin Quarter. And it was during this period that he supposedly contracted syphilis. Aupick disapproved of Baudelaire's actions and sent him to India in June of 1841. Baudelaire escaped and spent a few weeks in Mauritius and Réunion. After his return to France in February of 1842, he received his inheritance, which he spent lavishly on whatever he liked. His time on the islands had inspired his writing, and he wrote many poems for his *Les Fleurs du mal* collection (1857) between 1842 and 1846. Soon after, he met and fell in love with Jeanne Duval, the inspiration for 'Black Venus' in *Les Fleurs du mal*. His inheritance was quickly dwindling, so his mother and stepfather got a court order that limited Baudelaire's access to his money. In 1847, he published a novella called *La Fanfarlo*, modelling the main character after himself. Later that year, he became fascinated by Edgar Allen Poe's work, seeing striking similarities between Poe and himself. He began translating Poe's writing, publishing collections such as *Histoires extraordinaires* (1856) and *Eurêka* (1864). Baudelaire felt reaffirmed in his beliefs about poetry and art by Poe's opinions.

He became obsessed with Roman Catholicism in the 1850s, during which time he wrote about women like Apollonie Sabatier and the actress Marie Daubrun. Because of the influence of Poe's work and the recognition he earned from translating it, Baudelaire felt confident enough to publish his own work in the form of *Les Fleurs du mal* in 1857. Unfortunately, several of the poems from this collection were quickly banned for their religious and erotic themes. The next few years were difficult for Baudelaire as he struggled to come to terms with the failure of his publication. He wrote many of his most famous works during this time, but few were published. He moved back in with his mother in Honfleur in 1859 after his stepfather's death, writing poems such as 'Le Voyage' and 'Le Cygne' and essays like 'Salon de 1859.' He published another edition of *Les Fleurs du mal* in 1861.

After failing to join the French Academy, he focused on prose poetry, publishing twenty of them in *La Presse* (1862). In 1864, Baudelaire left for Brussels hoping to publish a collection of his writing., but while there he developed paralysis and aphasia, dying at the age of forty-six on 31 August 1867 in Paris. It was only after his death that he was established as one of the best French poets of the 19th century.

POEMS

La Géante

(tr. Arthur Symons)

From the time when Nature in her furious fancy
Conceived each day monstrosities obscene,
I had loved to live near a young Giantess of Necromancy,
Like a voluptuous cat before the knees of a Queen.

I had loved to see her body mix with her Soul's shame
And greaten in these terrible games of Vice,
And to divine if in her heart brooded a somber flame,
Before the moist sea-mists which swarm in her great eyes;

To wander over her huge forms – nature deforms us—
And to crawl over the slopes of her knees enormous,
And in summer when the unwholesome suns from the
    West's

Winds, weary, made her slumber hard by a fountain,
To sleep listlessly in the shadow of her superb breasts,
Like an hamlet that slumbers at the foot of a mountain.

Weeping and Wandering

(tr. Richard Herne Shepherd)

Say, Agatha, if at times your spirit turns
Far from the black sea of the city's mud,
To another ocean, where the splendour burns
All blue, and clear, and deep as maidenhood?
Say, Agatha, if your spirit thither turns?

The boundless sea consoles the weary mind!
What demon gave the sea – that chantress hoarse
To the huge organ of the chiding wind—
The function grand to rock us like a nurse?
The boundless ocean soothes the jaded mind!

O car and frigate, bear me far away,
For here our tears moisten the very clay.
Is't true that Agatha's sad heart at times
Says, Far from sorrows, from remorse, from crimes,
Remove me, car, and, frigate, bear away?

O perfumed paradise, how far removed,
Where 'neath a clear sky all is love and joy,
Where all we love is worthy to be loved,
And pleasure drowns the heart, but does not cloy.
O perfumed paradise, so far removed!

But the green paradise of childlike loves,
The walks, the songs, the kisses, and the flowers,
The violins dying behind the hills, the hours
Of evening and the wine-flasks in the groves.
But the green paradise of early loves,

The innocent paradise, full of stolen joys,
Is't farther off than ev'n the Indian main?
Can we recall it with out plaintive cries,
Or give it life, with silvery voice, again,
The innocent paradise, full of furtive joys?

Lesbos

(tr. Richard Herne Shepherd)

Mother of Latin sports and Greek delights.
Where kisses languishing or pleasureful,
Warm as the suns, as the water-melons cool,
Adorn the glorious days and sleepless nights.
Mother of Latin sports and Greek delights.

Lesbos, where kisses are as waterfalls
That fearless into gulfs unfathom'd leap,
Now run with sobs, now slip with gentle brawls,
Stormy and secret, manifold and deep;
Lesbos, where kisses are as waterfalls!
Lesbos, where Phryne Phryne to her draws,
Where ne'er a sigh did echoless expire.
As Paphos' equal thee the stars admire.
Nor Venus envies Sappho without cause!
Lesbos, where Phryne Phryne to her draws,

Lesbos, the land of warm and langorous nights.
Where by their mirrors seeking sterile good.
The girls with hollow eyes, in soft delights.
Caress the ripe fruits of their womanhood,
Lesbos, the land of warm and langorous nights.

Leave, leave old Plato's austere eye to frown;
Pardon is thine for kisses' sweet excess.
Queen of the land of amiable renown.
And for exhaustless subtleties of bliss.
Leave, leave old Plato's austere eye to frown.

Pardon is thine for the eternal pain
That on the ambitious hearts for ever lies.
Whom far from us the radiant smile could gain,
Seen dimly on the verge of other skies;
Pardon is thine for the eternal pain!
Which of the gods will dare thy judge to be.
And to condemn thy brow with labour pale.
Not having balanced in his golden scale
The flood of tears thy brooks pour'd in the sea?
Which of the gods will dare thy judge to be?

What boot the laws of just and of unjust?
Great-hearted virgins, honour of the isles,
Lo, your religion also is august,
And love at hell and heaven together smiles!
What boot the laws of just and of unjust?

For Lesbos chose me out from all my peers.
To sing the secret of her maids in flower.
Opening the mystery dark from childhood's hour
Of frantic laughters, mix'd with sombre tears;
For Lesbos chose me out from all my peers.

And since I from Leucate's top survey,
Like a sentinel with piercing eye and true.
Watching for brig and frigate night and day.
Whose distant outlines quiver in the blue.
And since I from Leucate's top survey.
To learn if kind and merciful the sea.
And midst the sobs that make the rock resound,
Brings back some eve to pardoning Lesbos, free
The worshipped corpse of Sappho, who made her bound
To learn if kind and merciful the sea!

Of her the man-like lover-poetess,
In her sad pallor more than Venus fair!
The azure eye yields to that black eye, where
The cloudy circle tells of the distress
Of her the man-like lover-poetess!

Fairer than Venus risen on the world.
Pouring the treasures of her aspect mild,
The radiance of her fair white youth unfurl'd
On Ocean old enchanted with his child;
Fairer than Venus risen on the world.

Of Sappho, who, blaspheming, died that day
When trampling on the rite and sacred creed.
She made her body fair the supreme prey
Of one whose pride punish'd the impious deed
Of Sappho who, blaspheming, died that day.
And since that time it is that Lesbos moans,
Andy spite the homage which the whole world pays.
Is drunk each night with cries of pain and groans,
Her desert shores unto the heavens do raise.
And since that time it is that Lesbos moans!

Don Juan in Hell

(tr. James Elroy Flecker)

The night Don Juan came to pay his fees
   To Charon, by the caverned water's shore,
A beggar, proud-eyed as Antisthenes,
   Stretched out his knotted fingers on the oar.

Mournful, with drooping breasts and robes unsewn
   The shapes of women swayed in ebon skies,
Trailing behind him with a restless moan
   Like cattle herded for a sacrifice.

Here, grinning for his wage, stood Sganarelle,
   And here Don Luis pointed, bent and dim,
To show the dead who lined the holes of Hell,
   This was that impious son who mocked at him.

The hollow-eyed, the chaste Elvira came,
   Trembling and veiled, to view her traitor spouse.
Was it one last bright smile she thought to claim,
   Such as made sweet the morning of his vows?

A great stone man rose like a tower on board,
   Stood at the helm and cleft the flood profound:
But the calm hero, leaning on his sword,
   Gazed back, and would not offer one look round.

Litany to Satan

(tr. James Elroy Flecker)

O grandest of the Angels, and most wise,
O fallen God, fate-driven from the skies,
Satan, at last take pity on our pain.

O first of exiles who endurest wrong,
Yet growest, in thy hatred, still more strong,
Satan, at last take pity on our pain!

O subterranean King, omniscient,
Healer of man's immortal discontent,
Satan, at last take pity on our pain.

To lepers and to outcasts thou dost show
That Passion is the Paradise below.
Satan, at last take pity on our pain.

Thou by thy mistress Death hast given to man
Hope, the imperishable courtesan.
Satan, at last take pity on our pain.

Thou givest to the Guilty their calm mien
Which damns the crowd around the guillotine
Satan, at last take pity on our pain.

Thou knowest the corners of the jealous Earth
Where God has hidden jewels of great worth.
Satan, at last take pity on our pain.

Thou dost discover by mysterious signs
Where sleep the buried people of the mines.
Satan, at last take pity on our pain.

Thou stretchest forth a saving hand to keep
Such men as roam upon the roofs in sleep.
Satan, at last take pity on our pain.

Thy power can make the halting Drunkard's feet
Avoid the peril of the surging street.
Satan, at last take pity on our pain.

Thou, to console our helplessness, didst plot
The cunning use of powder and of shot.
Satan, at last take pity on our pain.

Thy awful name is written as with pitch
On the unrelenting foreheads of the rich.
Satan, at last take pity on our pain.

In strange and hidden places thou dost move
Where women cry for torture in their love.
Satan, at last take pity on our pain.

Father of those whom God's tempestuous ire
Has flung from Paradise with sword and fire,
Satan, at last take pity on our pain.

Prayer
Satan, to thee be praise upon the Height
Where thou wast king of old, and in the night
Of Hell, where thou dost dream on silently.
Grant that one day beneath the Knowledge-tree,
When it shoots forth to grace thy royal brow,
My soul may sit, that cries upon thee now.

Élévation

(tr. Lewis Piaget Shanks)

above the valleys and above the meres,
above the mountains, woods, the clouds, the sea,
beyond the sun, beyond the canopy
of aether, and beyond the starry spheres,

o Mind, thou soarest easily and well,
and like a swimmer tranced in lifting seas,
thou cleavest all those deep immensities,
thrilled by a manly joy ineffable.

fly far beyond this fog of pestilence; fly!
go purge thy squalor in the loftier air;
go quaff the pure Olympian ichor where
clear fires fill the whole pellucid sky.

behind the cares, the dark anxieties
that on our sunless hours drag and drift,
happy is he whom sturdy pinions lift
in spirit, toward those fields of light and peace;

o happy he whose thoughts, unfurling wings,
leap skyward like the lark at morning's call,
– who soars above this life, resolving all
the speech of flowers and of voiceless things!

Correspondences

(tr. Lewis Piaget Shanks)

Nature's a fane where down each corridor
of living pillars, darkling whispers roll,
– a symbol-forest every pilgrim soul
must pierce, 'neath gazing eyes it knew before.

like echoes long that from afar rebound,
merged till one deep low shadowy note is born,
vast as the night or as the fires of morn,
sound calls to fragrance, colour calls to sound.

cool as an infant's brow some perfumes are,
softer than oboes, green as rainy leas;
others, corrupt, exultant, rich, unbar

wide infinities wherein we move at ease:
– musk, ambergris, frankincense, benjamin
chant all our soul or sense can revel in.

L'Ennemi

(tr. Lewis Piaget Shanks)

my youth was all a murky hurricane;
not oft did the suns of splendour burst the gloom;
so wild the lightning raged, so fierce the rain,
few crimson fruits my garden-close illume.

now I have touched the autumn of the mind,
I must repair and smooth the earth, to save
my little seed-plot, torn and undermined,
guttered and gaping like an open grave.

and will the flowers all my dreams implore
draw from this garden wasted like a shore
some rich mysterious power the storm imparts?

– o grief! o grief! time eats away our lives,
and the dark Enemy gnawing at our hearts
sucks from our blood the strength whereon he thrives!

L'Homme et la mer

(tr. Lewis Piaget Shanks)

love Ocean always, Man: ye both are free!
the Sea, thy mirror: thou canst find thy soul
in the unfurling billows' surging roll,
they mind's abyss is bitter as the sea.

thou doest rejoice thy mirrored face to pierce,
plunging, and clasp with eyes and arms; thy heart
at its own mutter oft forgets to start,
lulled by that plaint indomitably fierce.

discreet ye both are; both are taciturn:
Man, none has measured all thy dark abyss,
none, Sea, knows where thy hoarded treasure is,
so jealously your secrets ye inurn!

and yet for countless ages, trucelessly,
− o ruthless warriors! − ye have fought and striven:
brothers by lust for death and carnage driven,
twin wrestlers, gripped for all eternity!

Un Fantôme

(tr. Lewis Piaget Shanks)

I Les Tenebres
down in the unplumbed crypt of blight
where Fate abandoned me to die,
where falls no cheering ray; where I,
sole lodger of the sulky Night,

like artists blind God sets apart
in mockery – I paint the murk;
where, like a ghoulish cook at work,
I boil and munch upon my heart,

momently gleams, and grows apace,
a phantom languorously bright,
and by its dreamy Orient grace,

when it attains its radiant height,
at last I know the lovely thing:
'tis She! girl black yet glimmering.

II Le Parfum
how long, in silken favours, last
their prisoned scents! how greedily
we breathe the incense-grain, a sea
of fragrance, in cathedrals vast!

o deep enchanting sorcery!
in present joys to find the past!

'tis thus on cherished flesh amassed
Love culls the flower of memory.

her thick curled hair, like bags of musk
or living censers, left the dusk
with strange wild odours all astir,

and, from her lace and velvet busk,
– candid and girlish, over her,
hovered a heavy scent of fur.

III Le Cadre
as framing to a portrait gives
– though from a famous brush it be—
a magic full of mystery
secluding it from all that lives,

so gems, divans, gold, steel became
her beauty's border and attire;
no pomp obscured its perfect fire,
all seemed to serve her as a frame.

one even might have said she found
all sought to love her, for she drowned
in kisses of her silks and laces,

her fair nude body, all a-quiver,
and swift or slow, each pose would give her
a host of girlish simian graces.

IV Le Portrait

Death and Disease to ashes turn
all flames that wrapped our youth around.
of her soft eyes, so quick to burn,
her mouth, wherein my heart was drowned.

of her wild kisses' tyrannies,
her passion's blaze implacable—
drear heart! what now is left of these?
only a faded old pastel

dying, like me, in loneliness,
duller each day in every part,
stripped by Time's pinion merciless...

black murderer of life and art,
never shalt thou destroy in me
her, once my pride and ecstasy!

Je te donne ces vers afin que si mon nom

(tr. Lewis Piaget Shanks)

these lines to thee, that if my name should come
to some far harbour, on a favouring main,
and ride the gale to Time's Elysium,
with all its freight of dreams to fret the brain,

that thy report, like legends vague and vain,
may tire my reader as a mighty drum,
and linked in mystic union, may become
a symbol married to my haughty strain;

– accursèd one, to whom, from deepest skies
down to the Pit, naught, save my heart, replies!
– o thou who like a ghost impalpable

tramplest upon, serenely as a bonze
the stupid mortals who denied thy spell
– cold jet-eyed statue, angel cast in bronze!

Semper Eadem

(tr. Lewis Piaget Shanks)

you asked: 'what floods of gloom engulf you – strange
as creeping tides against a bare black wall?'
– when hearts once crush their grapes and close the
   grange,
life is an evil. secret known to all,

'tis but the common grief each man betrays
to all, as you your joy, in eyes or brow
so veil, my fair one, your inquiring gaze
and though your voice is low, be silent now!

be silent, simple soul! mouth always gay
with girlish laughter! more than Life, today,
Death binds our hearts with tenuous webs of doom;

let mine be drunken with the wine of lies,
o let me delve for dreams in those deep eyes
and slumber long beneath your eyebrows' gloom!

Tout Entière

(tr. Lewis Piaget Shanks)

this morning, to my chamber bare
and high, the Devil came to call,
and fain to trap me in a snare,
inquired: 'I would know, of all

— of all the beauties that compose
her spell profound, her subtle sway,
— of all the bits of black or rose
that form her lovely body, say

which is the sweetest?' — o my soul,
thou didst reply to the Abhorred:
naught can be taken from the whole
for every part is a perfect chord.

when all to me is ravishing,
I know not which gives most delight.
like dawn she is a dazzling thing,
yet she consoles me like the night;

too exquisite the harmonies
that all her lovely flesh affords,
for my poor mind to analyse
and note its many rhythmic chords.

o mystic interchange, whereby
my senses all are blent in one!
her breath is like a lullaby
and through her voice rich perfumes run!

L'Aube spirituelle

(tr. Lewis Piaget Shanks)

when to the drunkard's room the flushing East
comes with her comrade sharply-clawed, the Dream,
she wakens, by a dark avenging scheme,
an angel in the dull besotted beast.

deep vaults of inaccessible azure there,
before the dreamer sick with many a phasm,
open, abysmal as a beckoning chasm.
thus, deity, all pure clear light and air,

over the stupid orgy's reeking track .
– brighter and lovelier yet, thine image flies
in fluttering rays before my widening eyes.

the sun has turned the candles' flame to black;
even so, victorious always, thou art one
– resplendent spirit! – with the eternal sun!

Harmonie du soir

(tr. Lewis Piaget Shanks)

the hours approach when vibrant in the breeze,
a censer swoons to every swaying flower;
blown tunes and scents in turn enchant the bower;
languorous waltz of swirling fancies these!

a censer swoons in every swaying flower;
the quivering violins cry out, decrease;
languorous waltz of swirling fancies these!
mournful and fair the heavenly altars tower.

the quivering violins cry out, decrease;
like hearts of love the Void must overpower!
mournful and fair the heavenly altars tower.
the drowned sun bleeds in fast congealing seas.

a heart of love the Void must overpower
peers for a vanished day's last vestiges!
the drowned sun bleeds in fast congealing seas...
and like a Host thy flaming memories flower!

Le Poison

(tr. Lewis Piaget Shanks)

wine clothes the sordid walls of hovels old
with pomp no palace knows,
evokes long peristyles in pillared rows
from vaporous red and gold;
like sunset with her cloud-built porticoes.

and opium widens all that has no bourn
in its unbounded sea;
moments grow hours, pleasures cease to be
in souls that, overworn,
drown in its black abyss of lethargy.

dread poisons, but more dread the poisoned well
of thy green eyes accurst;
tarns where I watch my trembling soul, reversed
my dreams innumerable
throng to those bitter gulfs to slake their thirst.

dread magic, but thy mouth more dread than these:
its wine and hellebore
burn, floods of Lethe, in my bosom's core,
till winds of madness seize
and dash me swooning on Death's barren shore!

Ciel brouillé

(tr. Lewis Piaget Shanks)

thine eyes are veiled with vapour opaline;
– those eyes of mystery! – (azure, grey or green?)
cruel or soft in turn as dreams devise,
reflect the languor of the pallid skies.

thou'rt like these autumn days of silver-grey
whose magic melts the soul to tears: a day
when by a secret evil inly torn
the quivering nerves laugh drowsy wits to scorn.

thou art as fair as distant dales, where suns
of misty seasons leave their benisons...
how dazzling rich the dewy woodlands lie
flaming in sunlight from a ruffled sky!

o fateful woman! sky that lures and lours!
and shall I love thy snow, its frosty hours,
and learn to clutch from winter's iron gyves
new pleasure keen as cloven ice or knives?

Le Chat

(tr. Lewis Piaget Shanks)

I

she prowls around my shadowy brain
as though it were her dwelling-place
– a great soft beast of charming ways,
meowling in a mellow strain,

yet so discreetly all of her
angry or peaceful moods resound,
I scarcely hear their song profound
– her secret, rich, voluptuous purr.

o droning voice elegiac
creeping into my heart perverse
to drown it like a rippling verse
or potent aphrodisiac!

no torture that it cannot lull,
no ecstasy but it contains;
no phrase so long but its refrains
can voice it, wordless, wonderful.

nay, never master's bow divine,
rending my heart-strings like a sword,
rang, vibrant, in so rich a chord,
such royal harmony as thing,

as thine, mysterious puss, methinks,
feline seraphic, weird and strange,
spirit of subtlety and change,
melodious and lovely sphynx!

II
golden and brown, her tawny fur
secretes a scent of such delight
I breathe its fragrance till the night
when once my fingers fondle her.

she is the genius of the shrine;
no deed of mine and no desire
she does not judge, direct, inspire;
is she a fairy, or divine?

for when my amorous glances, fain
of her enchantment, slowly turn
and by their lode-stone drawn, discern
this prowling creature of my brain,

startled and marvelling I see
her glowing pupils cold and pale,
– clear harbour-lights no vapours veil—
like living opals, holding me.

Chant d'automne

(tr. Lewis Piaget Shanks)

I

soon shall we plunge 'neath winter's icy pall;
farewell, bright fires of too-brief July!
even now I hear the knell funereal
of falling fire-logs in the court close by.

once more on me shall winter all unroll:
wrath, hatred, shivering dread, Toil's cursèd vise,
and like the sun in his far hell, the pole,
my heart shall be a block of crimson ice.

I wait aghast each loud impending log;
thus, criminals 'neath rising gibbets cower.
o dreadful battering-ram! my soul, agog,
quivers and totters like a crumbling tower,

till to my dream the cradling echoes drum
like hammers madly finishing a bier.
– for whom? – June yesterday; now fall is come!
mysterious dirge, who has departed here?

II

I love your long green eyes of slumberous fire,
my sweet, but now all things are gall to me,
and naught, your room, your hearth nor your desire
is worth the sunlight shimmering on the sea.

yet love me, tender heart! a mother be
even to an ingrate, or a wicked one;
mistress or sister, be as sweet to me
as some brief autumn or a setting sun.

'twill not be long! the hungering tomb awaits!
ah! let me – brow at peace upon your knees—
savour, regretful of June's parching heats,
this balmy soft October, ere it flees!

La Cloche fêlée

(tr. Lewis Piaget Shanks)

'tis bitter joy, as winter evenings wear
before a smoking hearth which flames aghast,
to hear slow memories mounting from the past,
while church-bells pierce the pall of misty air.

blessèd the flawless bell, of metal rare,
the full-toned bourdon, void of rift and rust,
which like a guardsman faithful to his trust
hurls forth unfailingly its call to prayer!

my soul's a riven bell, that timidly
would fill the frozen night with melody,
but oft it falters, whisperingly weak

as, echoing over lakes of blood, a shriek
muffled by mounds of dead, from one who lies
moveless as they, though struggling till he dies.

Spleen

(tr. Lewis Piaget Shanks)

November, vexed with all the capital,
whelms in a death-chill from her gloomy urn
the cold pale dead beneath the graveyard wall,
the death-doomed who in dripping houses yearn.

Grimalkin prowls, a gaunt and scurvy ghoul,
seeking a softer lair for her sojourn;
along the eaves an ancient poet's soul
shivers and wails, a ghost no eyes discern.

the whining church-bell and the log a-sputter
repeat the rheumy clock's falsetto mutter;
while in a pack of cards, scent-filled and vile,

grim relic of a dropsical old maid,
the queen of spades and knave of hearts parade
their dead amours, with many an evil smile.

Spleen (2)

(tr. Lewis Piaget Shanks)

I hold more memories than a thousand years.

a chest of drawers crammed full of souvenirs,
accounts and love-notes, warrants, verses – where
from bills of sale fall coiling locks of hair—
guards not more secrets than my heart of woe,
a burial-vault whose coffins lie arow,
a potters' field that death has filled too soon.
– I am a graveyard hated by the moon,
where creeping worms trail slowly as remorse,
fiercely destroyed each belovèd corpse.

I am a room where faded roses lie
and gowns of perished fashions multiply,
with none but ladies in pastel to share
the musk from some old jar forgotten there.

no days so lame as all the days I know
while, crushed by years of ever-falling snow,
boredom, dull fruitage of my apathy,
waxes as vast as immortality.

henceforth, o living cells, ye sleep, a womb
faint shudders pierce, a cold grey cliff of doom
lost in a misty desert far away,
– a drowsy sphynx, forgot by all today,
uncharted avatar, whose tameless heart
sounds only when the day's last fires depart.

Spleen (3)

(tr. Lewis Piaget Shanks)

when low skies weightier than a coffin-lid
cast on the moaning soul their weary blight,
and from the whole horizon's murky grid
its grey light drips more dismal than the night;

when earth's a dungeon damp whose chill appals,
in which – a fluttering bat – my Hope, alone
buffets with timid wing the mouldering walls
and beats her head against the dome of stone;

when close as prison-bars, from overhead,
the clouds let fall the curtain of the rains,
and voiceless hordes of spiders come, to spread
their infamous cobwebs through our darkened brains,

explosively the bells begin to ring,
hurling their frightful clangour toward the sky,
as homeless spirits lost and wandering
might raise their indefatigable cry;

and ancient hearses through my soul advance
muffled and slow; my Hope, now pitiful,
weeps her defeat, and conquering Anguish plants
his great black banner on my cowering skull.

Alchimie de la douleur

(tr. Lewis Piaget Shanks)

one lights thee with his flame, another
puts in thee – Nature! – all his gloom!
what says to this man: lo! the tomb!
cries: life and splendour! to his brother.

o mage unknown whose powers assist
my art, and whom I always fear,
thou makest me a Midas – peer
of that most piteous alchemist;

for 'tis through thee I turn my gold
to iron, and in heaven behold
my hell: beneath her cloud-palls I

uncover corpses loved of old;
and where the shores celestial die
I carve vast tombs against the sky.

L'Avertisseur

(tr. Lewis Piaget Shanks)

each man who is a man must know
that yellow serpent in his heart,
ruling as on a throne apart,
that, when he says 'I will!' cries 'No!'

plunge in the fixed and frozen lies
of Satyr-maids' or nixies' eyes,
the Fang says: 'duty, not delight!'

engender children, plant a tree,
carve Paros, chisel poetry,
the Fang says: 'if thou die tonight?'

whatever plan or hope we grasp,
we cannot live one moment and
avoid the warning reprimand
of that intolerable asp.

Hymne

(tr. Lewis Piaget Shanks)

to her, my love and my delight,
my full heart's fiery ecstasy,
immortal goddess, heavenly sprite,
my pledge in immortality!

like briny air from ocean shores
through all my hours she drifts and clings,
and in my thirsty spirit pours
her love for everlasting things.

unchanging phial of perfume rare
drowning a shrine of love's delight,
forgotten censer smoking there
in secret through the shadowy night,

o love that shall defy decay,
how shall I truly utter thee?
o grain of musk hid far away
deep in my soul's eternity!

to her, my love and my delight,
my full heart's fiery ecstasy,
immortal goddess, heavenly sprite,
my pledge in immortality!

La Rançon

(tr. Lewis Piaget Shanks)

to pay our ransom, heaven-assigned,
two fields we have, whose fertile soil
we must make rich by constant toil
with the rude mattock of the mind;

to bring to bloom one single stem,
to wrest one sheaf of wheaten ears,
our brows, with bitter streaming tears,
must never cease to water them.

one field is Art, the other Love.
– and when that Day of Wrath-to-be,
the Day of Justice comes, if we
would satisfy the Judge above,

then we must point to barns abrim
with garnered hoards of golden grain,
and flowers fair enough to gain
the suffrage of the Seraphim.

L'Héautontimgrouménos

I'll strike thee without enmity
nor wrath, like butchers at the block,
like Moses when he smote the rock!
I'll make those eyelids gush for me

with springs of suffering, whose flow
shall slake the desert of my thirst;
– a salt flood, where my lust accurst,
with Hope to plump her sail, shall go

as from the port a pitching barge,
and in my heart they satiate
thy sobs I love shall fulminate
loud as a drum that beats a charge!

for am I not a clashing chord
in all Thy heavenly symphony,
thanks to this vulture Irony
that shakes and bites me always, Lord?

she's in my voice, the screaming elf!
my poisoned blood came all from her!
I am the mirror sinister
in which the vixen sees herself!

I am the wound and I the knife!
I am the blow I give, and feel!
I am the broken limbs, the wheel,
the hangman and the strangled life!

I am my heart's own vampire, for
God has forsaken me, and men,
these lips can never smile again,
but laugh they must, and evermore!

Le Squelette laboureur

(tr. Lewis Piaget Shanks)

I

in anatomic charts, upon
the parapets of dusty quays,
where coffined volumes lie at peace
like mummies dozing in the sun

– drawings where in the solemn zeal
of dexterous hands long turned to dust,
in things of sadness or disgust
have shown the beauty of the real—

we find – and then these lexicons
of cryptic horror grow complete!—
spading, like farmers, with their feet,
cadavers flayed and skeletons.

II

say, from the earth ye ransack there,
o patient serfs funereal,
with all your straining backbones, all
the strength of muscles peeled and bare,

tell me, o galley-slaves who moil,
from graves and charnel-houses torn,
whose barn ye hope to fill? what corn
will crown your long mysterious toil?

would ye (a proof in miniature
of some intolerable doom!)
teach us that even in the tomb
our promised sleep is not secure;

that graves, like all things else, are traps,
and nothingness another lie;
and that, although we mortals die,
'twill be our fate at last, perhaps,

in lands of loneliness complete,
to dig some rocky counterscarp,
pushing a heavy spade and sharp
beneath our naked bleeding feet?

Le Crépuscule du soir

(tr. Lewis Piaget Shanks)

'tis witching night, the criminal's ally;
it comes accomplice-like, wolf-soft; the sky
slowly is closing every giant door,
and man the rebel turns a beast once more.

o Night, delicious Night, they sigh for thee
– all those whose arms complain, and truly: we
have toiled today! her solace and her peace
Night brings to souls where cankering woes increase
– the self-willed scholar, nodding drowsily,
the workman bowed and hurrying bedward, free.
but now the evil demons of the air
wake heavily, like folk with many a care,
and, soaring, dash their heads on wall or blind.
among the gas-jets flickering in the wind
from every door, a hive that swarms a new,
pale Prostitution lights each avenue;
clearing her secret ways where lechers crawl
as might a foe who undermines a wall;
gorging on what we need, she nightly squirms
across the mire and darkness, like the worms.
the kitchens rattle 'round us everywhere,
playhouses roar and bands of music blare,
swindlers and bawds ally themselves to fleece
in wine shops, those who seek the cards' caprice,
while thieves, who truce nor mercy never knew,
will very soon resume their struggles too,

and gently force the door where treasure is
to feed themselves and dress their mistresses.

awake, my soul, in this grave hour of sin
and close thin ear to all its clamorous din.
now is the time when sick men's woes increase!
the murky night is throttling them; – they cease
to breathe, and sink into the Gulf, undone.
their groanings fill the poor house. – more than one
will seek no more at dusk his savoury bowl
beside the hearth, near some belovèd soul.

and most of these have never known the call
of home, nor had a hearth, nor lived at all!

L'Amour du mensonge

(tr. Lewis Piaget Shanks)

when I behold thee in thy nonchalance,
while from the dome the shards of music fall:
— thy feet that slowly weave a weary dance
— thy gaze a wearier flood engulfing all—

and when I watch thy brow so palely wan,
yet haunting in the gaslight's warm disguise,
— where evening's torches paint the rose of dawn
— thine eyes that hold me like a portrait's eyes

I cry: o rose bizarre, now bloomed afresh!
for regal memories crown her, towering, vast,
and all her heart's fruit, whose bruisèd flesh
is, like her body, riped for love at last.

art thou October fruit of sovereign wiles?
art thou an urn of tears for Sorrow's hours?
a fragrance wafting me to slumberous isles,
a roseleaf bed or funeral wreath of flowers?

some eyes are deep as though they always mourned
— eyes where no secret pearl of sorrow lies:
fair empty caskets by no gems adorned,
profound and bottomless as ye, o skies!

mere seeming this? but if thy seeming be
a balsam in my heart, with truth at war?
dull or indifferent, what were that to me?
hail, mask of art! thy beauty I adore.

Le Crépuscule du matin

(tr. Lewis Piaget Shanks)

across the barracks came the bugle-blare:
the wind of dawn made all the street-lamps flare.

it was the hour dreams of evil swarm
and dark-eyed striplings writhe in pallets warm;
when, like a bleeding, palpitating eye,
the lamp's a red blot on the daylight sly:
when the soul struggles, crushed and overborne
by cumbering flesh, like lamplight with the morn.
the air is full of quivering things; each flees
like slackening tear-drops cancelled by the breeze,
and poets tire of verse and maids of love.

spirals of smoke arose, the roofs above.
daughters of joy, wide-mouthed, with livid eye,
lay drowned in stupid sleep, their lips awry;
gaunt women, dragging breasts which hunger knew,
breathed on their embers and their fingers blue.

it was the hour that loads, by cold and dearth,
the woes of mothers waiting to give birth;
when, like a blood-choked sobbing cry, afar,
a cock's crow tore the air crepuscular
and each tall hive lay drowned in misty seas,
while from the poorhouse wall of secrecies
rang the last broken gasps of dying men.
outside, rakes worn with toil rode home again.

Dawn, in her green and rosy garment shivering,
down the deserted Seine came loitering,
and dark-browed Paris – toiler old and wise!—
caught up his shovel, rubbing both his eyes.

Le Vin du solitaire

(tr. Lewis Piaget Shanks)

the wildering glances of a harlot fair
seen gliding toward us like the silver wake
of undulant moonlight on the quivering lake
when Phoebe bathes her languorous beauty there;

the last gold coins a gambler's fingers hold;
the wanton kiss of love-worn Adeline,
the wheedling songs that leave the will supine
– like far-off cries of sorrow unconsoled—

all these, o bottle deep, were never worth
the pungent balsams in thy fertile girth
stored for the pious poet's thirsty heart;

thou pourest hope and youth and strength anew,
– and pride, this treasure of the beggar-crew,
that lifts us like triumphant gods, apart!

La Mort des artistes

(tr. Lewis Piaget Shanks)

how often must I shake my bells, and deign
to kiss thy brow debased, full travesty?
to pierce the mark, whose goal is mystery,
how oft, my quiver, waste thy darts in vain?

we shall exhaust our soul and subtle brain
and burst the bars of many a tyranny,
ere we shall glimpse the vast divinity
for which we burn and sob and burn again!

some too their idol never knew, and now,
flouted and branded with the brand of hell,
go beating fists of wrath on breast and brow;

one hope they know, strange, darkling citadel!
– can Death's new sunlight, streaming o'er the tomb,
lure the dead flower of their brain to bloom?

Le Léthé

(tr. Lewis Piaget Shanks)

come to my heart, cold viper-soul malign,
beloved tiger, hydra indolent;
long will I drag my hands incontinent
and quivering, through this vast loosed mane of thine;

long will I bury throbbing brow and head
among thy skirts all redolent of thee,
and breathe – a blighted flower of perfidy—
the fading odour of my passion dead.

I'll sleep, not live! I'll lose myself in sleep!
in slumber soft as Death's uncertain shore,
I'll sleep and sow my drowsy kisses o'er
thy polished coppery arms and bosom deep.

to drown my sobs and still my spirit – o!
no boon but thine abysmal bed avails;
poppied oblivion from thy mouth exhales
and through thy kisses floods of Lethe flow.

so to my doom, henceforward my desire,
I shall submit as one predestinate;
and like a martyr, calm, immaculate,
whose fervour prods again his flickering pyre,

I'll suck, to drown my hate's eternal smart,
Nepenthe, and good bitter hemlock brew,
from the sharp rose-buds of thy breast, anew,
thy breast that never did contain a heart.

A Former Life

(tr. Frank Pearce Sturm)

Long since, I lived beneath vast porticoes,
By many ocean-sunsets tinged and fired,
Where mighty pillars, in majestic rows,
Seemed like basaltic caves when day expired.

The rolling surge that mirrored all the skies
Mingled its music, turbulent and rich,
Solemn and mystic, with the colours which
The setting sun reflected in my eyes.

And there I lived amid voluptuous calms,
In splendours of blue sky and wandering wave,
Tended by many a naked, perfumed slave,

Who fanned my languid brow with waving palms.
They were my slaves – the only care they had
To know what secret grief had made me sad.

The Dance of Death

(tr. Frank Pearce Sturm)

Carrying bouquet, and handkerchief, and gloves,
Proud of her height as when she lived, she moves
With all the careless and high-stepping grace,
And the extravagant courtesan's thin face.

Was slimmer waist e'er in a ball-room wooed?
Her floating robe, in royal amplitude,
Palls in deep folds around a dry foot, shod
With a bright flower-like shoe that gems the sod.

The swarms that hum about her collar-bones
As the lascivious streams caress the stones,
Conceal from every scornful jest that flies,
Her gloomy beauty; and her fathomless eyes

Are made of shade and void; with flowery sprays
Her skull is wreathed artistically, and sways,
Feeble and weak, on her frail vertebræ.
O charm of nothing decked in folly! they

Who laugh and name you a Caricature,
They see not, they whom flesh and blood allure,
The nameless grace of every bleached, bare bone
That is most dear to me, tall skeleton!

Come you to trouble with your potent sneer
The feast of Life! or are you driven here,

To Pleasure's Sabbath, by dead lusts that stir
And goad your moving corpse on with a spur?

Or do you hope, when sing the violins,
And the pale candle-flame lights up our sins,
To drive some mocking nightmare far apart,
And cool the flame hell lighted in your heart?

Fathomless well of fault and foolishness!
Eternal alembic of antique distress!
Still o'er the curved, white trellis of your sides
The sateless, wandering serpent curls and glides.

And truth to tell, I fear lest you should find,
Among us here, no lover to your mind;
Which of these hearts beat for the smile you gave?
The charms of horror please none but the brave.

Your eyes' black gulf, where awful broodings stir,
Brings giddiness; the prudent reveller
Sees, while a horror grips him from beneath,
The eternal smile of thirty-two white teeth.

For he who has not folded in his arms
A skeleton, nor fed on graveyard charms,
Recks not of furbelow, or paint, or scent,
When Horror comes the way that Beauty went.

O irresistible, with fleshless face,
Say to these dancers in their dazzled race:
'Proud lovers with the paint above your bones,
Ye shall taste death, musk-scented skeletons!

Withered Antinoüs, dandies with plump faces,
Ye varnished cadavers, and grey Lovelaces,
Ye go to lands unknown and void of breath,
Drawn by the rumour of the Dance of Death.

From Seine's cold quays to Ganges' burning stream,
The mortal troupes dance onward in a dream;
They do not see, within the opened sky,
The Angel's sinister trumpet raised on high.

In every clime and under every sun,
Death laughs at ye, mad mortals, as ye run;
And oft perfumes herself with myrrh, like ye
And mingles with your madness, irony!'

The Beacons

(tr. Frank Pearce Sturm)

RUBENS, oblivious garden of indolence,
Pillow of cool flesh where no man dreams of love,
Where life flows forth in troubled opulence,
As airs in heaven and seas in ocean move,

LEONARD DA VINCI, sombre and fathomless glass,
Where lovely angels with calm lips that smile,
Heavy with mystery, in the shadow pass,
Among the ice and pines that guard some isle.

REMBRANDT, sad hospital that a murmuring fills,
Where one tall crucifix hangs on the walls,
Where every tear-drowned prayer some woe distils,
And one cold, wintry ray obliquely falls.

Strong MICHELANGELO, a vague far place
Where mingle Christs with pagan Hercules;
Thin phantoms of the great through twilight pace,
And tear their shroud with clenched hands void of ease.

The fighter's anger, the faun's impudence,
Thou makest of all these a lovely thing;
Proud heart, sick body, mind's magnificence:
PUGET, the convict's melancholy king.

WATTEAU, the carnival of illustrious hearts,
Fluttering like moths upon the wings of chance;

Bright lustres light the silk that flames and darts,
And pour down folly on the whirling dance.

GOYA, a nightmare full of things unknown;
The fœtus witches broil on Sabbath night;
Old women at the mirror; children lone
Who tempt old demons with their limbs delight.

DELACROIX, lake of blood ill angels haunt,
Where ever-green, o'ershadowing woods arise;
Under the surly heaven strange fanfares chaunt
And pass, like one of Weber's strangled sighs.

And malediction, blasphemy and groan,
Ecstasies, cries, Te Deums, and tears of brine,
Are echoes through a thousand labyrinths flown;
For mortal hearts an opiate divine;

A shout cried by a thousand sentinels,
An order from a thousand bugles tossed,
A beacon o'er a thousand citadels,
A call to huntsmen in deep woodlands lost.

It is the mightiest witness that could rise
To prove our dignity, O Lord, to Thee;
This sob that rolls from age to age, and dies
Upon the verge of Thy Eternity!

The Flask

(tr. Frank Pearce Sturm)

There are some powerful odours that can pass
Out of the stoppered flagon; even glass
To them is porous. Oft when some old box
Brought from the East is opened and the locks
And hinges creak and cry; or in a press
In some deserted house, where the sharp stress
Of odours old and dusty fills the brain;
An ancient flask is brought to light again,
And forth the ghosts of long-dead odours creep.
There, softly trembling in the shadows, sleep
A thousand thoughts, funereal chrysalides,
Phantoms of old the folding darkness hides,
Who make faint flutterings as their wings unfold,
Rose-washed and azure-tinted, shot with gold.

A memory that brings languor flutters here:
The fainting eyelids droop, and giddy Fear
Thrusts with both hands the soul towards the pit
Where, like a Lazarus from his winding-sheet,
Arises from the gulf of sleep a ghost
Of an old passion, long since loved and lost.
So I, when vanished from man's memory
Deep in some dark and sombre chest I lie.
An empty flagon they have cast aside,
Broken and soiled, the dust upon my pride,
Will be your shroud, beloved pestilence!
The witness of your might and virulence,
Sweet poison mixed by angels; bitter cup
Of life and death my heart has drunken up!

Reversibility

(tr. Frank Pearce Sturm)

Angel of gaiety, have you tasted grief?
Shame and remorse and sobs and weary spite,
And the vague terrors of the fearful night
That crush the heart up like a crumpled leaf?
Angel of gaiety, have you tasted grief?

Angel of kindness, have you tasted hate?
With hands clenched in the shade and tears of gall,
When Vengeance beats her hellish battle-call,
And makes herself the captain of our fate,
Angel of kindness, have you tasted hate?

Angel of health, did ever you know pain,
Which like an exile trails his tired footfalls
The cold length of the white infirmary walls,
With lips compressed, seeking the sun in vain?
Angel of health, did ever you know pain?

Angel of beauty, do you wrinkles know?
Know you the fear of age, the torment vile
Of reading secret horror in the smile
Of eyes your eyes have loved since long ago?
Angel of beauty, do you wrinkles know?

Angel of happiness, and joy, and light,
Old David would have asked for youth afresh
From the pure touch of your enchanted flesh;
I but implore your prayers to aid my plight,
Angel of happiness, and joy, and light.

The Eyes of Beauty

(tr. Frank Pearce Sturm)

You are a sky of autumn, pale and rose;
But all the sea of sadness in my blood
Surges, and ebbing, leaves my lips morose,
Salt with the memory of the bitter flood.

In vain your hand glides my faint bosom o'er,
That which you seek, beloved, is desecrate
By woman's tooth and talon; ah, no more
Seek in me for a heart which those dogs ate.

It is a ruin where the jackals rest,
And rend and tear and glut themselves and slay—
A perfume swims about your naked breast!

Beauty, hard scourge of spirits, have your way!
With flame-like eyes that at bright feasts have flared
Burn up these tatters that the beasts have spared!

To a Madonna

(tr. Frank Pearce Sturm)

(An Ex-Voto in the Spanish taste.)
Madonna, mistress. I would build for thee
An altar deep in the sad soul of me;
And in the darkest corner of my heart,
From mortal hopes and mocking eyes apart,
Carve of enamelled blue and gold a shrine
For thee to stand erect in, Image divine!
And with a mighty Crown thou shalt be crowned
Wrought of the gold of my smooth Verse, set round
With starry crystal rhymes; and I will make,
O mortal maid, a Mantle for thy sake,
And weave it of my jealousy, a gown
Heavy, barbaric, stiff, and weighted down
With my distrust, and broider round the hem
Not pearls, but all my tears in place of them.
And then thy wavering, trembling robe shall be
All the desires that rise and fall in me
From mountain-peaks to valleys of repose,
Kissing thy lovely body's white and rose.
For thy humiliated feet divine,
Of my Respect I'll make thee Slippers fine
Which, prisoning them within a gentle fold,
Shall keep their imprint like a faithful mould.
And if my art, unwearying and discreet,
Can make no Moon of Silver for thy feet
To have for Footstool, then thy heel shall rest
Upon the snake that gnaws within my breast,
Victorious Queen of whom our hope is born!

And thou shalt trample down and make a scorn
Of the vile reptile swollen up with hate.
And thou shalt see my thoughts, all consecrate,
Like candles set before thy flower-strewn shrine,
O Queen of Virgins, and the taper-shine
Shall glimmer star-like in the vault of blue,
With eyes of flame for ever watching you.
While all the love and worship in my sense
Will be sweet smoke of myrrh and frankincense.
Ceaselessly up to thee, white peak of snow,
My stormy spirit will in vapours go!

And last, to make thy drama all complete,
That love and cruelty may mix and meet,
I, thy remorseful torturer, will take
All the Seven Deadly Sins, and from them make
In darkest joy, Seven Knives, cruel-edged and keen,
And like a juggler choosing, O my Queen,
That spot profound whence love and mercy start,
I'll plunge them all within thy panting heart!

Bien Loin D'ici

(tr. Frank Pearce Sturm)

Here is the chamber consecrate,
Wherein this maiden delicate,
And enigmatically sedate,

Fans herself while the moments creep,
Upon her cushions half-asleep,
And hears the fountains plash and weep.

Dorothy's chamber undefiled.
The winds and waters sing afar
Their song of sighing strange and wild
To lull to sleep the petted child.

From head to foot with subtle care,
Slaves have perfumed her delicate skin
With odorous oils and benzoin.
And flowers faint in a corner there.

To a Brown Beggar-Maid

(tr. Frank Pearce Sturm)

White maiden with the russet hair,
Whose garments, through their holes, declare
That poverty is part of you,
And beauty too.

To me, a sorry bard and mean,
Your youthful beauty, frail and lean,
With summer freckles here and there,
Is sweet and fair.

Your sabots tread the roads of chance,
And not one queen of old romance
Carried her velvet shoes and lace
With half your grace.

In place of tatters far too short
Let the proud garments worn at Court
Fall down with rustling fold and pleat
About your feet;

In place of stockings, worn and old,
Let a keen dagger all of gold
Gleam in your garter for the eyes
Of roués wise;

Let ribbons carelessly untied
Reveal to us the radiant pride
Of your white bosom purer far
Than any star;

Let your white arms uncovered shine.
Polished and smooth and half divine;
And let your elfish fingers chase
With riotous grace

The purest pearls that softly glow.
The sweetest sonnets of Belleau,
Offered by gallants ere they fight
For your delight;

And many fawning rhymers who
Inscribe their first thin book to you
Will contemplate upon the stair
Your slipper fair;

And many a page who plays at cards,
And many lords and many bards,
Will watch your going forth, and burn
For your return;

And you will count before your glass
More kisses than the lily has;
And more than one Valois will sigh
When you pass by.

But meanwhile you are on the tramp,
Begging your living in the damp,
Wandering mean streets and alleys o'er,
From door to door;

And shilling bangles in a shop
Cause you with eager eyes to stop,
And I, alas, have not a sou
To give to you.

Then go, with no more ornament,
Pearl, diamond, or subtle scent,
Than your own fragile naked grace
And lovely face.

The Swan

(tr. Frank Pearce Sturm)

I

Andromache, I think of you! The stream,
The poor, sad mirror where in bygone days
Shone all the majesty of your widowed grief,
The lying Simoïs flooded by your tears,
Made all my fertile memory blossom forth
As I passed by the new-built Carrousel.
Old Paris is no more (a town, alas,
Changes more quickly than man's heart may change);
Yet in my mind I still can see the booths;
The heaps of brick and rough-hewn capitals;
The grass; the stones all over-green with moss;
The *débris*, and the square-set heaps of tiles.

There a menagerie was once outspread;
And there I saw, one morning at the hour
When toil awakes beneath the cold, clear sky,
And the road roars upon the silent air,
A swan who had escaped his cage, and walked
On the dry pavement with his webby feet,
And trailed his spotless plumage on the ground.
And near a waterless stream the piteous swan
Opened his beak, and bathing in the dust
His nervous wings, he cried (his heart the while
Filled with a vision of his own fair lake):
'O water, when then wilt thou come in rain?
Lightning, when wilt thou glitter?'

Sometimes yet
I see the hapless bird—strange, fatal myth—
Like him that Ovid writes of, lifting up
Unto the cruelly blue, ironic heavens,
With stretched, convulsive neck a thirsty face,
As though he sent reproaches up to God!

II
Paris may change; my melancholy is fixed.
New palaces, and scaffoldings, and blocks,
And suburbs old, are symbols all to me
Whose memories are as heavy as a stone.
And so, before the Louvre, to vex my soul,
The image came of my majestic swan
With his mad gestures, foolish and sublime,
As of an exile whom one great desire
Gnaws with no truce. And then I thought of you,
Andromache! torn from your hero's arms;
Beneath the hand of Pyrrhus in his pride;
Bent o'er an empty tomb in ecstasy;
Widow of Hector—wife of Helenus!
And of the negress, wan and phthisical,
Tramping the mud, and with her haggard eyes
Seeking beyond the mighty walls of fog
The absent palm-trees of proud Africa;
Of all who lose that which they never find;
Of all who drink of tears; all whom grey grief
Gives suck to as the kindly wolf gave suck;
Of meagre orphans who like blossoms fade.
And one old Memory like a crying horn

Sounds through the forest where my soul is lost....
I think of sailors on some isle forgotten;
Of captives; vanquished ... and of many more.

The Seven Old Men

(tr. Frank Pearce Sturm)

O swarming city, city full of dreams,
Where in full day the spectre walks and speaks;
Mighty colossus, in your narrow veins
My story flows as flows the rising sap.

One morn, disputing with my tired soul,
And like a hero stiffening all my nerves,
I trod a suburb shaken by the jar
Of rolling wheels, where the fog magnified
The houses either side of that sad street,
So they seemed like two wharves the ebbing flood
Leaves desolate by the river-side. A mist,
Unclean and yellow, inundated space—
A scene that would have pleased an actor's soul.
Then suddenly an aged man, whose rags
Were yellow as the rainy sky, whose looks
Should have brought alms in floods upon his head,
Without the misery gleaming in his eye,
Appeared before me; and his pupils seemed
To have been washed with gall; the bitter frost
Sharpened his glance; and from his chin a beard
Sword-stiff and ragged, Judas-like stuck forth.
He was not bent but broken: his backbone
Made a so true right angle with his legs,
That, as he walked, the tapping stick which gave
The finish to the picture, made him seem
Like some infirm and stumbling quadruped
Or a three-legged Jew. Through snow and mud

He walked with troubled and uncertain gait,
As though his sabots trod upon the dead,
Indifferent and hostile to the world.

His double followed him: tatters and stick
And back and eye and beard, all were the same;
Out of the same Hell, indistinguishable,
These centenarian twins, these spectres odd,
Trod the same pace toward some end unknown.
To what fell complot was I then exposed!
Humiliated by what evil chance?
For as the minutes one by one went by
Seven times I saw this sinister old man
Repeat his image there before my eyes!

Let him who smiles at my inquietude,
Who never trembled at a fear like mine,
Know that in their decrepitude's despite
These seven old hideous monsters had the mien
Of beings immortal.

Then, I thought, must I,
Undying, contemplate the awful eighth;
Inexorable, fatal, and ironic double;
Disgusting Phoenix, father of himself
And his own son! In terror then I turned
My back upon the infernal band, and fled
To my own place, and closed my door; distraught
And like a drunkard who sees all things twice,
With feverish troubled spirit, chilly and sick,
Wounded by mystery and absurdity!

In vain my reason tried to cross the bar,
The whirling storm but drove her back again;
And my soul tossed, and tossed, an outworn wreck,
Mastless, upon a monstrous, shoreless sea.

The Little Old Women

(tr. Frank Pearce Sturm)

Deep in the tortuous folds of ancient towns,
Where all, even horror, to enchantment turns,
I watch, obedient to my fatal mood,
For the decrepit, strange and charming beings,
The dislocated monsters that of old
Were lovely women – Laïs or Eponine!
Hunchbacked and broken, crooked though they be,
Let us still love them, for they still have souls.
They creep along wrapped in their chilly rags,
Beneath the whipping of the wicked wind,
They tremble when an omnibus rolls by,
And at their sides, a relic of the past,
A little flower-embroidered satchel hangs.
They trot about, most like to marionettes;
They drag themselves, as does a wounded beast;
Or dance unwillingly as a clapping bell
Where hangs and swings a demon without pity.
Though they be broken they have piercing eyes,
That shine like pools where water sleeps at night;
The astonished and divine eyes of a child
Who laughs at all that glitters in the world.
Have you not seen that most old women's shrouds
Are little like the shroud of a dead child?
Wise Death, in token of his happy whim,
Wraps old and young in one enfolding sheet.
And when I see a phantom, frail and wan,
Traverse the swarming picture that is Paris,
It ever seems as though the delicate thing

Trod with soft steps towards a cradle new.
And then I wonder, seeing the twisted form,
How many times must workmen change the shape
Of boxes where at length such limbs are laid?
These eyes are wells brimmed with a million tears;
Crucibles where the cooling metal pales—
Mysterious eyes that are strong charms to him
Whose life-long nurse has been austere Disaster.

II

The love-sick vestal of the old 'Frasciti';
Priestess of Thalia, alas! whose name
Only the prompter knows and he is dead;
Bygone celebrities that in bygone days
The Tivoli o'ershadowed in their bloom;
All charm me; yet among these beings frail
Three, turning pain to honey-sweetness, said
To the Devotion that had lent them wings:
'Lift me, O powerful Hippogriffe, to the skies'—
One by her country to despair was driven;
One by her husband overwhelmed with grief;
One wounded by her child, Madonna-like;
Each could have made a river with her tears.

III

Oft have I followed one of these old women,
One among others, when the falling sun
Reddened the heavens with a crimson wound—
Pensive, apart, she rested on a bench
To hear the brazen music of the band,
Played by the soldiers in the public park
To pour some courage into citizens' hearts,

On golden eves when all the world revives.
Proud and erect she drank the music in,
The lively and the warlike call to arms;
Her eyes blinked like an ancient eagle's eyes;
Her forehead seemed to await the laurel crown!

IV

Thus you do wander, uncomplaining Stoics,
Through all the chaos of the living town:
Mothers with bleeding hearts, saints, courtesans,
Whose names of yore were on the lips of all;
Who were all glory and all grace, and now
None know you; and the brutish drunkard stops,
Insulting you with his derisive love;
And cowardly urchins call behind your back.
Ashamed of living, withered shadows all,
With fear-bowed backs you creep beside the walls,
And none salute you, destined to loneliness!
Refuse of Time ripe for Eternity!
But I, who watch you tenderly afar,
With unquiet eyes on your uncertain steps,
As though I were your father, I – O wonder!—
Unknown to you taste secret, hidden joy.
I see your maiden passions bud and bloom,
Sombre or luminous, and your lost days
Unroll before me while my heart enjoys
All your old vices, and my soul expands
To all the virtues that have once been yours.
Ruined! and my sisters! O congenerate hearts,
Octogenarian Eves o'er whom is stretched
God's awful claw, where will you be to-morrow?

A Madrigal of Sorrow

(tr. Frank Pearce Sturm)

What do I care though you be wise?
Be sad, be beautiful; your tears
But add one more charm to your eyes,
As streams to valleys where they rise;
And fairer every flower appears

After the storm. I love you most
When joy has fled your brow downcast;
When your heart is in horror lost,
And o'er your present like a ghost
Floats the dark shadow of the past.

I love you when the teardrop flows,
Hot as blood, from your large eye;
When I would hush you to repose
Your heavy pain breaks forth and grows
Into a loud and tortured cry.

And then, voluptuousness divine!
Delicious ritual and profound!
I drink in every sob like wine,
And dream that in your deep heart shine
The pearls wherein your eyes were drowned.

I know your heart, which overflows
With outworn loves long cast aside,
Still like a furnace flames and glows,
And you within your breast enclose
A damnèd soul's unbending pride;

But till your dreams without release
Reflect the leaping flames of hell;
Till in a nightmare without cease
You dream of poison to bring peace,
And love cold steel and powder well;

And tremble at each opened door,
And feel for every man distrust,
And shudder at the striking hour—
Till then you have not felt the power
Of Irresistible Disgust.

My queen, my slave, whose love is fear,
When you awaken shuddering,
Until that awful hour be here,
You cannot say at midnight drear:
'I am your equal, O my King!'

An Allegory

(tr. Frank Pearce Sturm)

Here is a woman, richly clad and fair,
Who in her wine dips her long, heavy hair;
Love's claws, and that sharp poison which is sin,
Are dulled against the granite of her skin.
Death she defies, Debauch she smiles upon,
For their sharp scythe-like talons every one
Pass by her in their all-destructive play;
Leaving her beauty till a later day.
Goddess she walks; sultana in her leisure;
She has Mohammed's faith that heaven is pleasure,
And bids all men forget the world's alarms
Upon her breast, between her open arms.
She knows, and she believes, this sterile maid,
Without whom the world's onward dream would fade,
That bodily beauty is the supreme gift
Which may from every sin the terror lift.
Hell she ignores, and Purgatory defies;
And when black Night shall roll before her eyes,
She will look straight in Death's grim face forlorn,
Without remorse or hate – as one new born.

La Beatrice

(tr. Frank Pearce Sturm)

In a burnt, ashen land, where no herb grew,
I to the winds my cries of anguish threw;
And in my thoughts, in that sad place apart,
Pricked gently with the poignard o'er my heart.
Then in full noon above my head a cloud
Descended tempest-swollen, and a crowd
Of wild, lascivious spirits huddled there,
The cruel and curious demons of the air,
Who coldly to consider me began;
Then, as a crowd jeers some unhappy man,
Exchanging gestures, winking with their eyes—
I heard a laughing and a whispering rise:

'Let us at leisure contemplate this clown,
This shadow of Hamlet aping Hamlet's frown,
With wandering eyes and hair upon the wind.
Is't not a pity that this empty mind,
This tramp, this actor out of work, this droll,
Because he knows how to assume a rôle
Should dream that eagles and insects, streams and woods,
Stand still to hear him chaunt his dolorous moods?
Even unto us, who made these ancient things,
The fool his public lamentation sings.'

With pride as lofty as the towering cloud,
I would have stilled these clamouring demons loud,
And turned in scorn my sovereign head away
Had I not seen – O sight to dim the day!—

There in the middle of the troupe obscene
The proud and peerless beauty of my Queen!
She laughed with them at all my dark distress,
And gave to each in turn a vile caress.

The Soul Of Wine

(tr. Frank Pearce Sturm)

One eve in the bottle sang the soul of wine:
'Man, unto thee, dear disinherited,
I sing a song of love and light divine—
Prisoned in glass beneath my seals of red.

'I know thou labourest on the hill of fire,
In sweat and pain beneath a flaming sun,
To give the life and soul my vines desire,
And I am grateful for thy labours done.

'For I find joys unnumbered when I lave
The throat of man by travail long outworn,
And his hot bosom is a sweeter grave
Of sounder sleep than my cold caves forlorn.

'Hearest thou not the echoing Sabbath sound?
The hope that whispers in my trembling breast?
Thy elbows on the table! gaze around;
Glorify me with joy and be at rest.

'To thy wife's eyes I'll bring their long-lost gleam,
I'll bring back to thy child his strength and light,
To him, life's fragile athlete I will seem
Rare oil that firms his muscles for the fight.

'I flow in man's heart as ambrosia flows;
The grain the eternal Sower casts in the sod—
From our first loves the first fair verse arose,
Flower-like aspiring to the heavens and God!'

Gypsies Travelling

(tr. Frank Pearce Sturm)

The tribe prophetic with the eyes of fire
Went forth last night; their little ones at rest
Each on his mother's back, with his desire
Set on the ready treasure of her breast.

Laden with shining arms the men-folk tread
By the long wagons where their goods lie hidden;
They watch the heaven with eyes grown wearied
Of hopeless dreams that come to them unbidden.

The grasshopper, from out his sandy screen,
Watching them pass redoubles his shrill song;
Dian, who loves them, makes the grass more green,

And makes the rock run water for this throng
Of ever-wandering ones whose calm eyes see
Familiar realms of darkness yet to be.

A Landscape

(tr. Frank Pearce Sturm)

I would, when I compose my solemn verse,
Sleep near the heaven as do astrologers,
Near the high bells, and with a dreaming mind
Hear their calm hymns blown to me on the wind.

Out of my tower, with chin upon my hands,
I'll watch the singing, babbling human bands;
And see clock-towers like spars against the sky,
And heavens that bring thoughts of eternity;

And softly, through the mist, will watch the birth
Of stars in heaven and lamplight on the earth;
The threads of smoke that rise above the town;
The moon that pours her pale enchantment down.

Seasons will pass till Autumn fades the rose;
And when comes Winter with his weary snows,
I'll shut the doors and window-casements tight,
And build my faery palace in the night.

Then I will dream of blue horizons deep;
Of gardens where the marble fountains weep;
Of kisses, and of ever-singing birds—
A sinless Idyll built of innocent words.

And Trouble, knocking at my window-pane
And at my closet door, shall knock in vain;

I will not heed him with his stealthy tread,
Nor from my reverie uplift my head;

For I will plunge deep in the pleasure still
Of summoning the spring-time with my will,
Drawing the sun out of my heart, and there
With burning thoughts making a summer air.

The Voyage

(tr. Frank Pearce Sturm)

I

The world is equal to the child's desire
Who plays with pictures by his nursery fire—
How vast the world by lamplight seems! How small
When memory's eyes look back, remembering all!—

One morning we set forth with thoughts aflame,
Or heart o'erladen with desire or shame;
And cradle, to the song of surge and breeze,
Our own infinity on the finite seas.

Some flee the memory of their childhood's home;
And others flee their fatherland; and some,
Star-gazers drowned within a woman's eyes,
Flee from the tyrant Circe's witcheries;

And, lest they still be changed to beasts, take flight
For the embrasured heavens, and space, and light,
Till one by one the stains her kisses made
In biting cold and burning sunlight fade.

But the true voyagers are they who part
From all they love because a wandering heart
Drives them to fly the Fate they cannot fly;
Whose call is ever 'On!' – they know not why.

Their thoughts are like the clouds that veil a star;
They dream of change as warriors dream of war;

And strange wild wishes never twice the same:
Desires no mortal man can give a name.

II
We are like whirling tops and rolling balls—
For even when the sleepy night-time falls,
Old Curiosity still thrusts us on,
Like the cruel Angel who goads forth the sun.

The end of fate fades ever through the air,
And, being nowhere, may be anywhere
Where a man runs, hope waking in his breast,
For ever like a madman, seeking rest.

Our souls are wandering ships outwearied;
And one upon the bridge asks: 'What's ahead?'
The topman's voice with an exultant sound
Cries: 'Love and Glory!' – then we run aground.

Each isle the pilot signals when 'tis late,
Is El Dorado, promised us by fate—
Imagination, spite of her belief,
Finds, in the light of dawn, a barren reef.

Oh the poor seeker after lands that flee!
Shall we not bind and cast into the sea
This drunken sailor whose ecstatic mood
Makes bitterer still the water's weary flood?

Such is an old tramp wandering in the mire,
Dreaming the paradise of his own desire,
Discovering cities of enchanted sleep
Where'er the light shines on a rubbish heap.

III

Strange voyagers, what tales of noble deeds
Deep in your dim sea-weary eyes one reads!
Open the casket where your memories are,
And show each jewel, fashioned from a star;

For I would travel without sail or wind,
And so, to lift the sorrow from my mind,
Let your long memories of sea-days far fled
Pass o'er my spirit like a sail outspread.

What have you seen?

IV

'We have seen waves and stars,
And lost sea-beaches, and known many wars,
And notwithstanding war and hope and fear,
We were as weary there as we are here.

'The lights that on the violet sea poured down,
The suns that set behind some far-off town,
Lit in our hearts the unquiet wish to fly
Deep in the glimmering distance of the sky;

'The loveliest countries that rich cities bless,
Never contained the strange wild loveliness
By fate and chance shaped from the floating
    cloud—
And we were always sorrowful and proud!

'Desire from joy gains strength in weightier measure.
Desire, old tree who draw'st thy sap from pleasure,

Though thy bark thickens as the years pass by,
Thine arduous branches rise towards the sky;

'And wilt thou still grow taller, tree more fair
Than the tall cypress?
— Thus have we, with care,
Gathered some flowers to please your eager mood,
Brothers who dream that distant things are good!

'We have seen many a jewel-glimmering throne;
And bowed to Idols when wild horns were blown
In palaces whose faery pomp and gleam
To your rich men would be a ruinous dream;

'And robes that were a madness to the eyes;
Women whose teeth and nails were stained with dyes;
Wise jugglers round whose neck the serpent winds—'

V
And then, and then what more?

VI
'O childish minds!

'Forget not that which we found everywhere,
From top to bottom of the fatal stair,
Above, beneath, around us and within,
The weary pageant of immortal sin.

'We have seen woman, stupid slave and proud,
Before her own frail, foolish beauty bowed;

And man, a greedy, cruel, lascivious fool,
Slave of the slave, a ripple in a pool;

'The martyrs groan, the headsman's merry mood;
And banquets seasoned and perfumed with
  blood;
Poison, that gives the tyrant's power the slip;
And nations amorous of the brutal whip;

'Many religions not unlike our own,
All in full flight for heaven's resplendent throne;
And Sanctity, seeking delight in pain,
Like a sick man of his own sickness vain;

'And mad mortality, drunk with its own power,
As foolish now as in a bygone hour,
Shouting, in presence of the tortured Christ:
'I curse thee, mine own Image sacrificed.'

'And silly monks in love with Lunacy,
Fleeing the troops herded by destiny,
Who seek for peace in opiate slumber furled—
Such is the pageant of the rolling world!'

VII
O bitter knowledge that the wanderers gain!
The world says our own age is little and vain;
For ever, yesterday, to-day, to-morrow,
'Tis horror's oasis in the sands of sorrow.

Must we depart? If you can rest, remain;
Part, if you must. Some fly, some cower in vain,

Hoping that Time, the grim and eager foe,
Will pass them by; and some run to and fro

Like the Apostles or the Wandering Jew;
Go where they will, the Slayer goes there too!
And there are some, and these are of the wise,
Who die as soon as birth has lit their eyes.

But when at length the Slayer treads us low,
We will have hope and cry, "'Tis time to go!'
As when of old we parted for Cathay
With wind-blown hair and eyes upon the bay.

We will embark upon the Shadowy Sea,
Like youthful wanderers for the first time free—
Hear you the lovely and funereal voice
That sings: *O come all ye whose wandering joys*
Are set upon the scented Lotus flower,
For here we sell the fruit's miraculous boon;
Come ye and drink the sweet and sleepy power
Of the enchanted, endless afternoon.

VIII

O Death, old Captain, it is time, put forth!
We have grown weary of the gloomy north;
Though sea and sky are black as ink, lift sail!
Our hearts are full of light and will not fail.

O pour thy sleepy poison in the cup!
The fire within the heart so burns us up
That we would wander Hell and Heaven through,
Deep in the Unknown seeking something *new*!

The Sadness of the Moon

(tr. Frank Pearce Sturm)

The Moon more indolently dreams to-night
Than a fair woman on her couch at rest.
Caressing, with a hand distraught and light,
Before she sleeps, the contour of her breast.

Upon her silken avalanche of down,
Dying she breathes a long and swooning sigh;
And watches the white visions past her flown,
Which rise like blossoms to the azure sky.

And when, at times, wrapped in her languor deep,
Earthward she lets a furtive tear-drop flow,
Some pious poet, enemy of sleep,

Takes in his hollow hand the tear of snow
Whence gleams of iris and of opal start,
And hides it from the Sun, deep in his heart.

Exotic Perfume

(tr. Frank Pearce Sturm)

When with closed eyes in autumn's eves of gold
I breathe the burning odours of your breast,
Before my eyes the hills of happy rest
Bathed in the sun's monotonous fires, unfold.

Islands of Lethe where exotic boughs
Bend with their burden of strange fruit bowed down.
Where men are upright, maids have never grown
Unkind, but bear a light upon their brows.

Led by that perfume to these lands of ease,
I see a port where many ships have flown
With sails outwearied of the wandering seas;

While the faint odours from green tamarisks blown,
Float to my soul and in my senses throng,
And mingle vaguely with the sailor's song.

Beauty

(tr. Frank Pearce Sturm)

I am as lovely as a dream in stone,
And this my heart where each finds death in turn,
Inspires the poet with a love as lone
As clay eternal and as taciturn.

Swan-white of heart, a sphinx no mortal knows,
My throne is in the heaven's azure deep;
I hate all movements that disturb my pose,
I smile not ever, neither do I weep.

Before my monumental attitudes,
That breathe a soul into the plastic arts,
My poets pray in austere studious moods,

For I, to fold enchantment round their hearts,
Have pools of light where beauty flames and dies,
The placid mirrors of my luminous eyes.

The Balcony

(tr. Frank Pearce Sturm)

Mother of memories, mistress of mistresses,
O thou, my pleasure, thou, all my desire,
Thou shalt recall the beauty of caresses,
The charm of evenings by the gentle fire,
Mother of memories, mistress of mistresses!

The eves illumined by the burning coal,
The balcony where veiled rose-vapour clings—
How soft your breast was then, how sweet your soul!
Ah, and we said imperishable things,
Those eves illumined by the burning coal.

Lovely the suns were in those twilights warm,
And space profound, and strong life's pulsing flood,
In bending o'er you, queen of every charm,
I thought I breathed the perfume in your blood.
The suns were beauteous in those twilights warm.

The film of night flowed round and over us,
And my eyes in the dark did your eyes meet;
I drank your breath, ah! sweet and poisonous,
And in my hands fraternal slept your feet—
Night, like a film, flowed round and over us.

I can recall those happy days forgot,
And see, with head bowed on your knees, my past.
Your languid beauties now would move me not

Did not your gentle heart and body cast
The old spell of those happy days forgot.

Can vows and perfumes, kisses infinite,
Be reborn from the gulf we cannot sound;
As rise to heaven suns once again made bright
After being plunged in deep seas and profound?
Ah, vows and perfumes, kisses infinite!

The Sick Muse

(tr. Frank Pearce Sturm)

Poor Muse, alas, what ails thee, then, to-day?
Thy hollow eyes with midnight visions burn,
Upon thy brow in alternation play,
Folly and Horror, cold and taciturn.

Have the green lemure and the goblin red,
Poured on thee love and terror from their urn?
Or with despotic hand the nightmare dread
Deep plunged thee in some fabulous Minturne?

Would that thy breast where so deep thoughts arise,
Breathed forth a healthful perfume with thy sighs;
Would that thy Christian blood ran wave by wave

In rhythmic sounds the antique numbers gave,
When Phœbus shared his alternating reign
With mighty Pan, lord of the ripening grain.

The Venal Muse

(Frank Pearce Sturm)

Muse of my heart, lover of palaces,
When January comes with wind and sleet,
During the snowy eve's long wearinesses,
Will there be fire to warm thy violet feet?

Wilt thou reanimate thy marble shoulders
In the moon-beams that through the window fly?
Or when thy purse dries up, thy palace moulders,
Reap the far star-gold of the vaulted sky?

For thou, to keep thy body to thy soul,
Must swing a censer, wear a holy stole,
And chaunt Te Deums with unbelief between.

Or, like a starving mountebank, expose
Thy beauty and thy tear-drowned smile to those
Who wait thy jests to drive away thy spleen.

The Evil Monk

(tr. Frank Pearce Sturm)

The ancient cloisters on their lofty walls
Had holy Truth in painted frescoes shown,
And, seeing these, the pious in those halls
Felt their cold, lone austereness less alone.

At that time when Christ's seed flowered all around,
More than one monk, forgotten in his hour,
Taking for studio the burial-ground,
Glorified Death with simple faith and power.

And my soul is a sepulchre where I,
Ill cenobite, have spent eternity:
On the vile cloister walls no pictures rise.

O when may I cast off this weariness,
And make the pageant of my old distress
For these hands labour, pleasure for these eyes?

The Temptation

(*tr. Frank Pearce Sturm*)

The Demon, in my chamber high,
This morning came to visit me,
And, thinking he would find some fault,
He whispered: 'I would know of thee

Among the many lovely things
That make the magic of her face,
Among the beauties, black and rose,
That make her body's charm and grace,

Which is most fair?' Thou didst reply
To the Abhorred, O soul of mine:
'No single beauty is the best
When she is all one flower divine.

When all things charm me I ignore
Which one alone brings most delight;
She shines before me like the dawn,
And she consoles me like the night.

The harmony is far too great,
That governs all her body fair,
For impotence to analyse
And say which note is sweetest there.

O mystic metamorphosis!
My senses into one sense flow—
Her voice makes perfume when she speaks,
Her breath is music faint and low!'

The Irreparable

(tr. Frank Pearce Sturm)

I

Can we suppress the old Remorse
Who bends our heart beneath his stroke,
Who feeds, as worms feed on the corse,
Or as the acorn on the oak?
Can we suppress the old Remorse?

Ah, in what philtre, wine, or spell,
May we drown this our ancient foe,
Destructive glutton, gorging well,
Patient as the ants, and slow?
What wine, what philtre, or what spell?

Tell it, enchantress, if you can,
Tell me, with anguish overcast,
Wounded, as a dying man,
Beneath the swift hoofs hurrying past.
Tell it, enchantress, if you can,

To him the wolf already tears
Who sees the carrion pinions wave,
This broken warrior who despairs
To have a cross above his grave—
This wretch the wolf already tears.

Can one illume a leaden sky,
Or tear apart the shadowy veil
Thicker than pitch, no star on high,

Not one funereal glimmer pale
Can one illume a leaden sky?

Hope lit the windows of the Inn,
But now that shining flame is dead;
And how shall martyred pilgrims win
Along the moonless road they tread?
Satan has darkened all the Inn!

Witch, do you love accursèd hearts?
Say, do you know the reprobate?
Know you Remorse, whose venomed darts
Make souls the targets for their hate?
Witch, do you know accursèd hearts?

The Might-have-been with tooth accursed
Gnaws at the piteous souls of men,
The deep foundations suffer first,
And all the structure crumbles then
Beneath the bitter tooth accursed.

II

Often, when seated at the play,
And sonorous music lights the stage,
I see the frail hand of a Fay
With magic dawn illume the rage
Of the dark sky. Oft at the play

A being made of gauze and fire
Casts to the earth a Demon great.
And my heart, whence all hopes expire,
Is like a stage where I await,
In vain, the Fay with wings of fire!

The Living Flame

(tr. Frank Pearce Sturm)

They pass before me, these Eyes full of light,
Eyes made magnetic by some angel wise;
The holy brothers pass before my sight,
And cast their diamond fires in my dim eyes.

They keep me from all sin and error grave,
They set me in the path whence Beauty came;
They are my servants, and I am their slave,
And all my soul obeys the living flame.

Beautiful Eyes that gleam with mystic light
As candles lighted at full noon; the sun
Dims not your flame phantastical and bright.

You sing the dawn; they celebrate life done;
Marching you chaunt my soul's awakening hymn,
Stars that no sun has ever made grow dim!

Sonnet of Autumn

(tr. Frank Pearce Sturm)

They say to me, thy clear and crystal eyes:
'Why dost thou love me so, strange lover mine?'
Be sweet, be still! My heart and soul despise
All save that antique brute-like faith of thine;

And will not bare the secret of their shame
To thee whose hand soothes me to slumbers long,
Nor their black legend write for thee in flame!
Passion I hate, a spirit does me wrong.

Let us love gently. Love, from his retreat,
Ambushed and shadowy, bends his fatal bow,
And I too well his ancient arrows know:

Crime, horror, folly. O pale marguerite,
Thou art as I, a bright sun fallen low,
O my so white, my so cold Marguerite.

The Remorse of the Dead

(tr. Frank Pearce Sturm)

O shadowy Beauty mine, when thou shalt sleep
In the deep heart of a black marble tomb;
When thou for mansion and for bower shalt keep
Only one rainy cave of hollow gloom;

And when the stone upon thy trembling breast,
And on thy straight sweet body's supple grace,
Crushes thy will and keeps thy heart at rest,
And holds those feet from their adventurous race;

Then the deep grave, who shares my reverie,
(For the deep grave is aye the poet's friend)
During long nights when sleep is far from thee,

Shall whisper: 'Ah, thou didst not comprehend
The dead wept thus, thou woman frail and weak'—
And like remorse the worm shall gnaw thy cheek.

The Ghost

(tr. Frank Pearce Sturm)

Softly as brown-eyed Angels rove
I will return to thy alcove,
And glide upon the night to thee,
Treading the shadows silently.

And I will give to thee, my own,
Kisses as icy as the moon,
And the caresses of a snake
Cold gliding in the thorny brake.

And when returns the livid morn
Thou shalt find all my place forlorn
And chilly, till the falling night.

Others would rule by tenderness
Over thy life and youthfulness,
But I would conquer thee by fright!

The Sky

(tr. Frank Pearce Sturm)

Where'er he be, on water or on land,
Under pale suns or climes that flames enfold;
One of Christ's own, or of Cythera's band,
Shadowy beggar or Crœsus rich with gold;

Citizen, peasant, student, tramp; whate'er
His little brain may be, alive or dead;
Man knows the fear of mystery everywhere,
And peeps, with trembling glances, overhead.

The heaven above? A strangling cavern wall;
The lighted ceiling of a music-hall
Where every actor treads a bloody soil—

The hermit's hope; the terror of the sot;
The sky: the black lid of the mighty pot
Where the vast human generations boil!

Spleen

(tr. Frank Pearce Sturm)

I'm like some king in whose corrupted veins
Flows aged blood; who rules a land of rains;
Who, young in years, is old in all distress;
Who flees good counsel to find weariness
Among his dogs and playthings, who is stirred
Neither by hunting-hound nor hunting-bird;
Whose weary face emotion moves no more
E'en when his people die before his door.
His favourite Jester's most fantastic wile
Upon that sick, cruel face can raise no smile;
The courtly dames, to whom all kings are good,
Can lighten this young skeleton's dull mood
No more with shameless toilets. In his gloom
Even his lilied bed becomes a tomb.
The sage who takes his gold essays in vain
To purge away the old corrupted strain,
His baths of blood, that in the days of old
The Romans used when their hot blood grew cold,
Will never warm this dead man's bloodless pains,
For green Lethean water fills his veins.

The Owls

(tr. Frank Pearce Sturm)

Under the overhanging yews,
The dark owls sit in solemn state.
Like stranger gods; by twos and twos
Their red eyes gleam. They meditate.

Motionless thus they sit and dream
Until that melancholy hour
When, with the sun's last fading gleam,
The nightly shades assume their power.

From their still attitude the wise
Will learn with terror to despise
All tumult, movement, and unrest;

For he who follows every shade,
Carries the memory in his breast,
Of each unhappy journey made.

Music

(tr. Frank Pearce Sturm)

Music doth oft uplift me like a sea
Towards my planet pale,
Then through dark fogs or heaven's infinity
I lift my wandering sail.

With breast advanced, drinking the winds that flee,
And through the cordage wail,
I mount the hurrying waves night hides from me
Beneath her sombre veil.

I feel the tremblings of all passions known
To ships before the breeze;
Cradled by gentle winds, or tempest-blown

I pass the abysmal seas
That are, when calm, the mirror level and fair
Of my despair!

Contemplation

(tr. Frank Pearce Sturm)

Thou, O my Grief, be wise and tranquil still,
The eve is thine which even now drops down,
To carry peace or care to human will,
And in a misty veil enfolds the town.

While the vile mortals of the multitude,
By pleasure, cruel tormentor, goaded on,
Gather remorseful blossoms in light mood—
Grief, place thy hand in mine, let us be gone

Far from them. Lo, see how the vanished years,
In robes outworn lean over heaven's rim;
And from the water, smiling through her tears,

Remorse arises, and the sun grows dim;
And in the east, her long shroud trailing light,
List, O my grief, the gentle steps of Night.

The Ideal

(tr. *Frank Pearce Sturm*)

Not all the beauties in old prints vignetted,
The worthless products of an outworn age,
With slippered feet and fingers castanetted,
The thirst of hearts like my heart can assuage.

To Gavarni, the poet of chloroses,
I leave his troupes of beauties sick and wan;
I cannot find among these pale, pale roses,
The red ideal mine eyes would gaze upon.

Lady Macbeth, the lovely star of crime,
The Greek poet's dream born in a northern clime—
Ah, she could quench my dark heart's deep desiring;

Or Michelangelo's dark daughter Night,
In a strange posture dreamily admiring
Her beauty fashioned for a giant's delight!

Mist and Rain

(tr. Frank Pearce Sturm)

Autumns and winters, springs of mire and rain,
Seasons of sleep, I sing your praises loud,
For thus I love to wrap my heart and brain
In some dim tomb beneath a vapoury shroud

In the wide plain where revels the cold wind,
Through long nights when the weathercock whirls round,
More free than in warm summer day my mind
Lifts wide her raven pinions from the ground.

Unto a heart filled with funereal things
That since old days hoar frosts have gathered on,
Naught is more sweet, O pallid, queenly springs,
Than the long pageant of your shadows wan,
Unless it be on moonless eves to weep
On some chance bed and rock our griefs to sleep.

Sunset

(tr. Frank Pearce Sturm)

Fair is the sun when first he flames above,
Flinging his joy down in a happy beam;
And happy he who can salute with love
The sunset far more glorious than a dream.

Flower, stream, and furrow! – I have seen them all
In the sun's eye swoon like one trembling heart—
Though it be late let us with speed depart
To catch at least one last ray ere it fall!

But I pursue the fading god in vain,
For conquering Night makes firm her dark domain,
Mist and gloom fall, and terrors glide between,

And graveyard odours in the shadow swim,
And my faint footsteps on the marsh's rim,
Bruise the cold snail and crawling toad unseen.

The Corpse

(tr. Frank Pearce Sturm)

Remember, my Beloved, what thing we met
By the roadside on that sweet summer day;
There on a grassy couch with pebbles set,
A loathsome body lay.

The wanton limbs stiff-stretched into the air,
Steaming with exhalations vile and dank,
In ruthless cynic fashion had laid bare
The swollen side and flank.

On this decay the sun shone hot from heaven
As though with chemic heat to broil and burn,
And unto Nature all that she had given
A hundredfold return.

The sky smiled down upon the horror there
As on a flower that opens to the day;
So awful an infection smote the air,
Almost you swooned away.

The swarming flies hummed on the putrid side,
Whence poured the maggots in a darkling
    stream,
That ran along these tatters of life's pride
With a liquescent gleam.

And like a wave the maggots rose and fell,
The murmuring flies swirled round in busy strife:

It seemed as though a vague breath came to swell
And multiply with life

The hideous corpse. From all this living world
A music as of wind and water ran,
Or as of grain in rhythmic motion swirled
By the swift winnower's fan.

And then the vague forms like a dream died out,
Or like some distant scene that slowly falls
Upon the artist's canvas, that with doubt
He only half recalls.

A homeless dog behind the boulders lay
And watched us both with angry eyes forlorn,
Waiting a chance to come and take away
The morsel she had torn.

And you, even you, will be like this drear thing,
A vile infection man may not endure;
Star that I yearn to! Sun that lights my spring!
O passionate and pure!

Yes, such will you be, Queen of every grace!
When the last sacramental words are said;
And beneath grass and flowers that lovely face
Moulders among the dead.

Then, O Beloved, whisper to the worm
That crawls up to devour you with a kiss,
That I still guard in memory the dear form
Of love that comes to this!

The Accursed

(tr. Frank Pearce Sturm)

Like pensive herds at rest upon the sands,
These to the sea-horizons turn their eyes;
Out of their folded feet and clinging hands
Bitter sharp tremblings and soft languors rise.

Some tread the thicket by the babbling stream,
Their hearts with untold secrets ill at ease;
Calling the lover of their childhood's dream,
They wound the green bark of the shooting trees.

Others like sisters wander, grave and slow,
Among the rocks haunted by spectres thin,
Where Antony saw as larvæ surge and flow
The veined bare breasts that tempted him to sin.

Some, when the resinous torch of burning wood
Flares in lost pagan caverns dark and deep,
Call thee to quench the fever in their blood,
Bacchus, who singest old remorse to sleep!

Then there are those the scapular bedights,
Whose long white vestments hide the whip's red
    stain,
Who mix, in sombre woods on lonely nights,
The foam of pleasure with the tears of pain.

O virgins, demons, monsters, martyrs! ye
Who scorn whatever actual appears;

Saints, satyrs, seekers of Infinity,
So full of cries, so full of bitter tears;

Ye whom my soul has followed into hell,
I love and pity, O sad sisters mine,
Your thirsts unquenched, your pains no tongue can tell,
And your great hearts, those urns of love divine!

The Wine of Lovers

(tr. Frank Pearce Sturm)

Space rolls to-day her splendour round!
Unbridled, spurless, without bound,
Mount we upon the wings of wine
For skies fantastic and divine!

Let us, like angels tortured by
Some wild delirious phantasy,
Follow the far-off mirage born
In the blue crystal of the morn.

And gently balanced on the wing
Of the wild whirlwind we will ride,
Rejoicing with the joyous thing.

My sister, floating side by side,
Fly we unceasing whither gleams
The distant heaven of my dreams.

The Death of Lovers

(tr. Frank Pearce Sturm)

There shall be couches whence faint odours rise,
Divans like sepulchres, deep and profound;
Strange flowers that bloomed beneath diviner skies
The death-bed of our love shall breathe around.

And guarding their last embers till the end,
Our hearts shall be the torches of the shrine,
And their two leaping flames shall fade and blend
In the twin mirrors of your soul and mine.

And through the eve of rose and mystic blue
A beam of love shall pass from me to you,
Like a long sigh charged with a last farewell;

And later still an angel, flinging wide
The gates, shall bring to life with joyful spell
The tarnished mirrors and the flames that died.

The Death of the Poor

(tr. Frank Pearce Sturm)

Death is consoler and Death brings to life;
The end of all, the solitary hope;
We, drunk with Death's elixir, face the strife,
Take heart, and mount till eve the weary slope.

Across the storm, the hoar-frost, and the snow,
Death on our dark horizon pulses clear;
Death is the famous hostel we all know,
Where we may rest and sleep and have good cheer.

Death is an angel whose magnetic palms
Bring dreams of ecstasy and slumberous calms
To smooth the beds of naked men and poor.

Death is the mystic granary of God;
The poor man's purse; his fatherland of yore;
The Gate that opens into heavens untrod!

The Benediction

(tr. Frank Pearce Sturm)

When by the high decree of powers supreme,
The Poet came into this world outworn,
She who had borne him, in a ghastly dream,
Clenched blasphemous hands at God, and cried in scorn:

'O rather had I borne a writhing knot
Of unclean vipers, than my breast should nurse
This vile derision, of my joy begot
To be my expiation and my curse!

'Since of all women thou hast made of me
Unto my husband a disgust and shame;
Since I may not cast this monstrosity,
Like an old love-epistle, to the flame;

'I will pour out thine overwhelming hate
On this the accursed weapon of thy spite;
This stunted tree I will so desecrate
That not one tainted bud shall see the light!'

So foaming with the foam of hate and shame,
Blind unto God's design inexorable,
With her own hands she fed the purging flame
To crimes maternal consecrate in hell.

Meanwhile beneath an Angel's care unseen
The child disowned grows drunken with the sun;
His food and drink, though they be poor and mean,
With streams of nectar and ambrosia run.

Speaking to clouds and playing with the wind,
With joy he sings the sad Way of the Rood;
His shadowing pilgrim spirit weeps behind
To see him gay as birds are in the wood.

Those he would love looked sideways and with fear,
Or, taking courage from his aspect mild,
Sought who should first bring to his eye the tear,
And spent their anger on the dreaming child.

With all the bread and wine the Poet must eat
They mingled earth and ash and excrement,
All things he touched were spurned beneath their feet;
They mourned if they must tread the road he went.

His wife ran crying in the public square:
'Since he has found me worthy to adore,
Shall I not be as antique idols were,
With gold and with bright colours painted o'er?

'I will be drunk with nard and frankincense.
With myrrh, and knees bowed down, and flesh and wine.
Can I not, smiling, in his love-sick sense,
Usurp the homage due to beings divine?

'I will lay on him my fierce, fragile hand
When I am weary of the impious play;
For well these harpy talons understand
To furrow to his heart their crimson way.

'I'll tear the red thing beating from his breast,
To cast it with disdain upon the ground,

Like a young bird torn trembling from the nest—
His heart shall go to gorge my favourite hound.'

To the far heaven, where gleams a splendid throne,
The Poet uplifts his arms in calm delight,
And the vast beams from his pure spirit flown,
Wrap all the furious peoples from his sight:

'Thou, O my God, be blest who givest pain,
The balm divine for each imperfect heart,
The strong pure essence cleansing every stain
Of sin that keeps us from thy joys apart.

'Among the numbers of thy legions blest,
I know a place awaits the poet there;
Him thou hast bid attend the eternal feast
That Thrones and Virtues and Dominions share.

'I know the one thing noble is a grief
Withstanding earth's and hell's destructive tooth,
And I, through all my dolorous life and brief,
To gain the mystic crown, must cry the truth.

'The jewels lost in Palmyra of old,
Metals unknown, pearls of the outer sea,
Are far too dim to set within the gold
Of the bright crown that Time prepares for me.

'For it is wrought of pure unmingled light,
Dipped in the white flame whence all flame is born—
The flame that makes all eyes, though diamond-bright,
Seem obscure mirrors, darkened and forlorn.'

Robed in a Silken Robe

(tr. Frank Pearce Sturm)

Robed in a silken robe that shines and shakes,
She seems to dance whene'er she treads the sod,
Like the long serpent that a fakir makes
Dance to the waving cadence of a rod.

As the sad sand upon the desert's verge,
Insensible to mortal grief and strife;
As the long weeds that float among the surge,
She folds indifference round her budding life.

Her eyes are carved of minerals pure and cold,
And in her strange symbolic nature where
An angel mingles with the sphinx of old,

Where all is gold and steel and light and air,
For ever, like a vain star, unafraid
Shines the cold hauteur of the sterile maid.

POEMS IN PROSE

The Stranger

(tr. Frank Pearce Sturm)

Tell me, enigmatic man, whom do you love best?
Your father, your mother, your sister, or your brother?
   'I have neither father, nor mother, nor sister,
   nor brother.'
Your friends, then?
   'You use a word that until now has had no meaning
   for me.'
Your country?
   'I am ignorant of the latitude in which it is situated.'
Then Beauty?
   'Her I would love willingly, goddess and immortal.'
Gold?
   'I hate it as you hate your God.'
What, then, extraordinary stranger, do you love?
   'I love the clouds—the clouds that pass—yonder—the
   marvellous clouds.'

Every Man His Chimæra

(tr. Frank Pearce Sturm)

Beneath a broad grey sky, upon a vast and dusty plain
devoid of grass, and where not even a nettle or a thistle
was to be seen, I met several men who walked bowed
down to the ground.

Each one carried upon his back an enormous Chimæra
as heavy as a sack of flour or coal, or as the equipment of
a Roman foot-soldier.

But the monstrous beast was not a dead weight, rather
she enveloped and oppressed the men with her powerful
and elastic muscles, and clawed with her two vast talons
at the breast of her mount. Her fabulous head reposed
upon the brow of the man like one of those horrible
casques by which ancient warriors hoped to add to the
terrors of the enemy.

I questioned one of the men, asking him why they
went so. He replied that he knew nothing, neither he
nor the others, but that evidently they went somewhere,
since they were urged on by an unconquerable desire
to walk.

Very curiously, none of the wayfarers seemed to be
irritated by the ferocious beast hanging at his neck and
cleaving to his back: one had said that he considered it as
a part of himself. These grave and weary faces bore
witness to no despair. Beneath the splenetic cupola of the
heavens, their feet trudging through the dust of an earth
as desolate as the sky, they journeyed onwards with the
resigned faces of men condemned to hope for ever. So the
train passed me and faded into the atmosphere of the

horizon at the place where the planet unveils herself to the curiosity of the human eye.

During several moments I obstinately endeavoured to comprehend this mystery; but irresistible Indifference soon threw herself upon me, nor was I more heavily dejected thereby than they by their crushing Chimæras.

Venus and the Fool

(tr. Frank Pearce Sturm)

How admirable the day! The vast park swoons beneath the burning eye of the sun, as youth beneath the lordship of love.

There is no rumour of the universal ecstasy of all things. The waters themselves are as though drifting into sleep. Very different from the festivals of humanity, here is a silent revel.

It seems as though an ever-waning light makes all objects glimmer more and more, as though the excited flowers burn with a desire to rival the blue of the sky by the vividness of their colours; as though the heat, making perfumes visible, drives them in vapour towards their star.

Yet, in the midst of this universal joy, I have perceived one afflicted thing.

At the feet of a colossal Venus, one of those motley fools, those willing clowns whose business it is to bring laughter upon kings when weariness or remorse possesses them, lies wrapped in his gaudy and ridiculous garments, coiffed with his cap and bells, huddled against the pedestal, and raises towards the goddess his eyes filled with tears.

And his eyes say: 'I am the last and most alone of all mortals, inferior to the meanest of animals in that I am denied either love or friendship. Yet I am made, even I, for the understanding and enjoyment of immortal Beauty. O Goddess, have pity upon my sadness and my frenzy.'

The implacable Venus gazed into I know not what distances with her marble eyes.

Intoxication

(tr. Frank Pearce Sturm)

One must be for ever drunken: that is the sole question
of importance. If you would not feel the horrible burden
of Time that bruises your shoulders and bends you to the
earth, you must be drunken without cease. But how? With
wine, with poetry, with virtue, with what you please. But
be drunken. And if sometimes, on the steps of a palace,
on the green grass by a moat, or in the dull loneliness of
your chamber, you should waken up, your intoxication
already lessened or gone, ask of the wind, of the wave, of
the star, of the bird, of the time-piece; ask of all that flees,
all that sighs, all that revolves, all that sings, all that
speaks, ask of these the hour; and wind and wave and star
and bird and time-piece will answer you: 'It is the hour
to be drunken! Lest you be the martyred slaves of Time,
intoxicate yourselves, be drunken without cease! With
wine, with poetry, with virtue, or with what you will.'

The Gifts of the Moon

(tr. Frank Pearce Sturm)

The Moon, who is caprice itself, looked in at the window as you slept in your cradle, and said to herself: 'I am well pleased with this child.'

And she softly descended her stairway of clouds and passed through the window-pane without noise. She bent over you with the supple tenderness of a mother and laid her colours upon your face. Therefrom your eyes have remained green and your cheeks extraordinarily pale. From contemplation of your visitor your eyes are so strangely wide; and she so tenderly wounded you upon the breast that you have ever kept a certain readiness to tears.

In the amplitude of her joy, the Moon filled all your chamber as with a phosphorescent air, a luminous poison; and all this living radiance thought and said: 'You shall be for ever under the influence of my kiss. You shall love all that loves me and that I love: clouds, and silence, and night; the vast green sea; the unformed and multitudinous waters; the place where you are not; the lover you will never know; monstrous flowers, and perfumes that bring madness; cats that stretch themselves swooning upon the piano and lament with the sweet, hoarse voices of women.

'And you shall be loved of my lovers, courted of my courtesans. You shall be the Queen of men with green eyes, whose breasts also I have wounded in my nocturnal caress: men that love the sea, the immense green ungovernable sea; the unformed and multitudinous waters; the place where they are not; the woman they will never know; sinister flowers that seem to bear the incense of some unknown religion; perfumes that trouble the will; and all savage and voluptuous animals, images of their own folly.'

And that is why I am couched at your feet, O spoiled child, beloved and accursed, seeking in all your being the reflection of that august divinity, that prophetic god-mother, that poisonous nurse of all lunatics.

The Invitation to the Voyage

(tr. Frank Pearce Sturm)

It is a superb land, a country of Cockaigne, as they say, that I dream of visiting with an old friend. A strange land, drowned in our northern fogs, that one might call the East of the West, the China of Europe; a land patiently and luxuriously decorated with the wise, delicate vegetations of a warm and capricious phantasy.

A true land of Cockaigne, where all is beautiful, rich, tranquil, and honest; where luxury is pleased to mirror itself in order; where life is opulent, and sweet to breathe; from whence disorder, turbulence, and the unforeseen are excluded; where happiness is married to silence; where even the food is poetic, rich and exciting at the same time; where all things, my beloved, are like you.

Do you know that feverish malady that seizes hold of us in our cold miseries; that nostalgia of a land unknown; that anguish of curiosity? It is a land which resembles you, where all is beautiful, rich, tranquil and honest, where phantasy has built and decorated an occidental China, where life is sweet to breathe, and happiness married to silence. It is there that one would live; there that one would die.

Yes, it is there that one must go to breathe, to dream, and to lengthen one's hours by an infinity of sensations. A musician has written the 'Invitation to the Waltz'; where is he who will write the 'Invitation to the Voyage,' that one may offer it to his beloved, to the sister of his election?

Yes, it is in this atmosphere that it would be good to live, – yonder, where slower hours contain more thoughts, where the clocks strike the hours of happiness with a more profound and significant solemnity.

Upon the shining panels, or upon skins gilded with a sombre opulence, beatified paintings have a discreet life, as calm and profound as the souls of the artists who created them.

The setting suns that colour the rooms and salons with so rich a light, shine through veils of rich tapestry, or through high leaden-worked windows of many compartments. The furniture is massive, curious, and bizarre, armed with locks and secrets, like profound and refined souls. The mirrors, the metals, the ail ver work and the china, play a mute and mysterious symphony for the eyes; and from all things, from the corners, from the chinks in the drawers, from the folds of drapery, a singular perfume escapes, a Sumatran *revenez*-y, which is like the soul of the apartment.

A true country of Cockaigne, I have said; where all is rich, correct and shining, like a beautiful conscience, or a splendid set of silver, or a medley of jewels. The treasures of the world flow there, as in the house of a laborious man who has well merited the entire world. A singular land, as superior to others as Art is superior to Nature; where Nature is made over again by dream; where she is corrected, embellished, refashioned.

Let them seek and seek again, let them extend the limits of their happiness for ever, these alchemists who work with flowers! Let them offer a prize of sixty or a hundred thousand florins to whosoever can solve their ambitious problems! As for me, I have found my *black tulip* and my *blue dahlia*!

Incomparable flower, tulip found at last, symbolical

dahlia, it is there, is it not, in this so calm and dreamy land that you live and blossom? Will you not there be framed in your proper analogy, and will you not be mirrored, to speak like the mystics, in your own *correspondence?*

Dreams!—always dreams! and the more ambitious and delicate the soul, the farther from possibility is the dream. Every man carries within him his dose of natural opium, incessantly secreted and renewed, and, from birth to death, how many hours can we count that have been filled with positive joy, with successful and decided action? Shall we ever live in and become a part of the picture my spirit has painted, the picture that resembles you?

These treasures, furnishings, luxury, order, perfumes and miraculous flowers, are you. You again are the great rivers and calm canals. The enormous ships drifting beneath their loads of riches, and musical with the sailors' monotonous song, are my thoughts that sleep and stir upon your breast. You take them gently to the sea that is Infinity, reflecting the profundities of the sky in the limpid waters of your lovely soul; – and when, outworn by the surge and gorged with the products of the Orient, the ships come back to the ports of home, they are still my thoughts, grown rich, that have returned to you from Infinity.

What is Truth?

(tr. Frank Pearce Sturm)

I once knew a certain Benedicta whose presence ailed the air with the ideal and whose eyes spread abroad the desire of grandeur, of beauty, of glory, and of all that makes man believe in immortality.

But this miraculous maiden was too beautiful for long life, so she died soon after I knew her first, and it was I myself who entombed her, upon a day when spring swung her censer even in the burial-ground. It was I myself who entombed her, fast closed in a coffin of perfumed wood, as uncorruptible as the coffers of India.

And, as my eyes rested upon the spot where my treasure lay hidden, I became suddenly aware of a little being who singularly resembled the dead; and who, stamping the newly-turned earth with a curious and hysterical violence, burst into laughter, and said: 'It is I, the true Benedicta! It is I, the notorious drab! As the punishment of your folly and blindness you shall love me as I truly am.'

But I, furious, replied: 'No!' The better to emphasise my refusal I struck the ground so violently with my foot that my leg was thrust up to the knee in the recent grave, and I, like a wolf in a trap, was caught perhaps for ever in the Grave of the Ideal.

Already!

(tr. Frank Pearce Sturm)

A hundred times already the sun had leaped, radiant or saddened, from the immense cup of the sea whose rim could scarcely be seen; a hundred times it had again sunk, glittering or morose, into its mighty bath of twilight. For many days we had contemplated the other side of the firmament, and deciphered the celestial alphabet of the antipodes. And each of the passengers sighed and complained. One had said that the approach of land only exasperated their sufferings. 'When, then,' they said, 'shall we cease to sleep a sleep broken by the surge, troubled by a wind that snores louder than we? When shall we be able to eat at an unmoving table?'

There were those who thought of their own firesides, who regretted their sullen, faithless wives, and their noisy progeny. All so doted upon the image of the absent land, that I believe they would have eaten grass with as much enthusiasm as the beasts.

At length a coast was signalled, and on approaching we saw a magnificent and dazzling land. It seemed as though the music of life flowed therefrom in a vague murmur; and the banks, rich with all kinds of growths, breathed, for leagues around, a delicious odour of flowers and fruits.

Each one therefore was joyful; his evil humour left him. Quarrels were forgotten, reciprocal wrongs forgiven, the thought of duels was blotted out of the memory, and rancour fled away like smoke.

I alone was sad, inconceivably sad. Like a priest from

whom one has torn his divinity, I could not, without heartbreaking bitterness, leave this so monstrously seductive ocean, this sea so infinitely various in its terrifying simplicity, which seemed to contain in itself and represent by its joys, and attractions, and angers, and smiles, the moods and agonies and ecstasies of all souls that have lived, that live, and that shall yet live.

In saying good-bye to this incomparable beauty I felt as though I had been smitten to death; and that is why when each of my companions said: 'At last!' I could only cry '*Already!*'

Here meanwhile was the land, the land with its noises, its passions, its commodities, its festivals: a land rich and magnificent, full of promises, that sent to us a mysterious perfume of rose and musk, and from whence the music of life flowed in an amorous murmuring.

The Double Chamber

(tr. Frank Pearce Sturm)

A chamber that is like a reverie; a chamber truly *spiritual*, where the stagnant atmosphere is lightly touched with rose and blue.

There the soul bathes itself in indolence made odorous with regret and desire. There is some sense of the twilight, of things tinged with blue and rose: a dream of delight during an eclipse. The shape of the furniture is elongated, low, languishing; one would think it endowed with the somnambulistic vitality of plants and minerals.

The tapestries speak an inarticulate language, like the flowers, the skies, the dropping suns.

There are no artistic abominations upon the walls. Compared with the pure dream, with an impression unanalysed, definite art, positive art, is a blasphemy. Here all has the sufficing lucidity and the delicious obscurity of music.

An infinitesimal odour of the most exquisite choice, mingled with a floating humidity, swims in this atmosphere where the drowsing spirit is lulled by the sensations one feels in a hothouse.

The abundant muslin flows before the windows and the couch, and spreads out in snowy cascades. Upon the couch lies the Idol, ruler of my dreams. But why is she here? – who has brought her? – what magical power has installed her upon this throne of delight and reverie? What matter – she is there; and I recognise her.

These indeed are the eyes whose flame pierces the twilight; the subtle and terrible mirrors that I recognise by their horrifying malice. They attract, they dominate, they devour the sight of whomsoever is imprudent enough to look at them. I have often studied them; these Black Stars that compel curiosity and admiration.

To what benevolent demon, then, do I owe being thus surrounded with mystery, with silence, with peace, and sweet odours? O beatitude! the thing we name life, even in its most fortunate amplitude, has nothing in common with this supreme life with which I am now acquainted, which I taste minute by minute, second by second.

Not so! Minutes are no more; seconds are no more. Time has vanished, and Eternity reigns – an Eternity of delight.

A heavy and terrible knocking reverberates upon the door, and, as in a hellish dream, it seems to me as though I had received a blow from a mattock.

Then a Spectre enters: it is an usher who comes to torture me in the name of the Law; an infamous concubine who comes to cry misery and to add the trivialities of her life to the sorrow of mine; or it may be the errand-boy of an editor who comes to implore the remainder of a manuscript.

The chamber of paradise, the Idol, the ruler of dreams, the Sylphide, as the great René said; all this magic has vanished at the brutal knocking of the Spectre.

Horror; I remember, I remember! Yes, this kennel, this habitation of eternal weariness, is indeed my own. There is my senseless furniture, dusty and tattered; the dirty fireplace without a flame or an ember; the sad windows where the raindrops have traced runnels in the dust; the manuscripts, erased or unfinished; the almanac with the sinister days marked off with a pencil!

And this perfume of another world, whereof I
intoxicated myself with a so perfected sensitiveness; alas,
its place is taken by an odour of stale tobacco smoke,
mingled with I know not what nauseating mustiness.
Now one breathes here the rankness of desolation.

In this narrow world, narrow and yet full of disgust, a
single familiar object smiles at me: the phial of laudanum:
old and terrible love; like all loves, alas! fruitful in caresses
and treacheries.

Yes, Time has reappeared; Time reigns a monarch now;
and with the hideous Ancient has returned all his
demoniacal following of Memories, Regrets, Tremors,
Fears, Dolours, Nightmares, and twittering nerves.

I assure you that the seconds are strongly and solemnly
accentuated now; and each, as it drips from the
pendulum, says: 'I am Life: intolerable, implacable Life!'

There is not a second in mortal life whose mission it
is to bear good news: the good news that brings the
inexplicable tear to the eye.

Yes, Time reigns; Time has regained his brutal mastery.
And he goads me, as though I were a steer, with his
double goad: 'Whoa, thou fool! Sweat, then, thou slave!
Live on, thou damnèd!'

At One O'clock in the Morning

(tr. Frank Pearce Sturm)

Alone at last! Nothing is to be heard but the rattle of a
few tardy and tired-out cabs. There will be silence now, if
not repose, for several hours at least. At last the tyranny of
the human face has disappeared – I shall not suffer except
alone. At last it is permitted me to refresh myself in a
bath of shadows. But first a double turn of the key in the
lock. It seems to me that this turn of the key will deepen
my solitude and strengthen the barriers which actually
separate me from the world.

A horrible life and a horrible city! Let us run over the
events of the day. I have seen several literary men; one of
them wished to know if he could get to Russia by land
(he seemed to have an idea that Russia was an island); I
have disputed generously enough with the editor of a
review, who to each objection replied: 'We take the part
of respectable people,' which implies that every other
paper but his own is edited by a knave; I have saluted
some twenty people, fifteen of them unknown to me; and
shaken hands with a like number, without having taken
the precaution of first buying gloves; I have been driven
to kill time, during a shower, with a mountebank, who
wanted me to design for her a costume as Venusta; I have
made my bow to a theatre manager, who said: 'You will
do well, perhaps, to interview Z; he is the heaviest,
foolishest, and most celebrated of all my authors; with
him perhaps you will be able to come to something. See
him, and then we'll see,' I have boasted (why?) of several
villainous deeds I never committed, and indignantly

denied certain shameful things I accomplished with joy, certain misdeeds of fanfaronade, crimes of human respect; I have refused an easy favour to a friend and given a written recommendation to a perfect fool. Heavens! it's well ended.

Discontented with myself and with everything and everybody else, I should be glad enough to redeem myself and regain my self-respect in the silence and solitude.

Souls of those whom I have loved, whom I have sung, fortify me; sustain me; drive away the lies and the corrupting vapours of this world; and Thou, Lord my God, accord me so much grace as shall produce some beautiful verse to prove to myself that I am not the last of men, that I am not inferior to those I despise.

The Confiteor of the Artist

(tr. Frank Pearce Sturm)

How penetrating is the end of an autumn day! Ah, yes, penetrating enough to be painful even; for there are certain delicious sensations whose vagueness does not prevent them from being intense; and none more keen than the perception of the Infinite. He has a great delight who drowns his gaze in the immensity of sky and sea. Solitude, silence, the incomparable chastity of the azure – a little sail trembling upon the horizon, by its very littleness and isolation imitating my irremediable existence – the melodious monotone of the surge – all these things thinking through me and I through them (for in the grandeur of the reverie the Ego is swiftly lost); they think, I say, but musically and picturesquely, without quibbles, without syllogisms, without deductions.

These thoughts, as they arise in me or spring forth from external objects, soon become always too intense. The energy working within pleasure creates an uneasiness, a positive suffering. My nerves are too tense to give other than clamouring and dolorous vibrations.

And now the profundity of the sky dismays me; its limpidity exasperates me. The insensibility of the sea, the immutability of the spectacle, revolt me. Ah, must one eternally suffer, for ever be a fugitive from Beauty?

Nature, pitiless enchantress, ever-victorious rival, leave me! Tempt my desires and my pride no more. The contemplation of Beauty is a duel where the artist screams with terror before being vanquished.

The Thyrsus

(tr. Frank Pearce Sturm)

TO FRANZ LISZT

What is a thyrsus? According to the moral and poetical sense, it is a sacerdotal emblem in the hand of the priests or priestesses celebrating the divinity of whom they are the interpreters and servants. But physically it is no more than a baton, a pure staff, a hop-pole, a vine-prop; dry, straight, and hard. Around this baton, in capricious meanderings, stems and flowers twine and wanton; these, sinuous and fugitive; those, hanging like bells or inverted cups. And an astonishing complexity disengages itself from this complexity of tender or brilliant lines and colours. Would not one suppose that the curved line and the spiral pay their court to the straight line, and twine about it in a mute adoration? Would not one say that all these delicate corollæ, all these calices, explosions of odours and colours, execute a mystical dance around the hieratic staff? And what imprudent mortal will dare to decide whether the flowers and the vine branches have been made for the baton, or whether the baton is not but a pretext to set forth the beauty of the vine branches and the flowers?

The thyrsus is the symbol of your astonishing duality, O powerful and venerated master, dear bacchanal of a mysterious and impassioned Beauty. Never a nymph excited by the mysterious Dionysius shook her thyrsus over the heads of her companions with as much energy as your genius trembles in the hearts of your brothers.

The baton is your will: erect, firm, unshakeable; the flowers are the wanderings of your fancy around it: the feminine element encircling the masculine with her illusive dance. Straight line and arabesque – intention and expression – the rigidity of the will and the suppleness of the word – a variety of means united for a single purpose – the all-powerful and indivisible amalgam that is genius – what analyst will have the detestable courage to divide or to separate you?

Dear Liszt, across the fogs, beyond the flowers, in towns where the pianos chant your glory, where the printing-house translates your wisdom; in whatever place you be, in the splendour of the Eternal City or among the fogs of the dreamy towns that Cambrinus consoles; improvising rituals of delight or ineffable pain, or giving to paper your abstruse meditations; singer of eternal pleasure and pain, philosopher, poet, and artist, I offer you the salutation of immortality!

The Marksman

(tr. Frank Pearce Sturm)

As the carriage traversed the wood he bade the driver
draw up in the neighbourhood of a shooting gallery,
saying that he would like to have a few shots to kill time.
Is not the slaying of the monster Time the most ordinary
and legitimate occupation of man?—So he gallantly
offered his hand to his dear, adorable, and execrable wife;
the mysterious woman to whom he owed so many
pleasures, so many pains, and perhaps also a great part of
his genius.

Several bullets went wide of the proposed mark, one
of them flew far into the heavens, and as the charming
creature laughed deliriously, mocking the clumsiness of
her husband, he turned to her brusquely and said:
'Observe that doll yonder, to the right, with its nose in
the air, and with so haughty an appearance. Very well,
dear angel, I will *imagine to myself that it is you!*'

He closed both eyes and pulled the trigger. The doll
was neatly decapitated.

Then, bending towards his dear, adorable, and
execrable wife, his inevitable and pitiless muse, he kissed
her respectfully upon the hand, and added, 'Ah, dear
angel, how I thank you for my skill!'

The Shooting-Range and the Cemetery

(tr. Frank Pearce Sturm)

'Cemetery View Inn' – 'A queer sign,' said our traveller to himself; 'but it raises a thirst! Certainly the keeper of this inn appreciates Horace and the poet pupils of Epicurus. Perhaps he even apprehends the profound philosophy of those old Egyptians who had no feast without its skeleton, or some emblem of life's brevity.'

He entered: drank a glass of beer in presence of the tombs; and slowly smoked a cigar. Then, his phantasy driving him, he went down into the cemetery, where the grass was so tall and inviting; so brilliant in the sunshine.

The light and heat, indeed, were so furiously intense that one had said the drunken sun wallowed upon a carpet of flowers that had fattened upon the corruption beneath.

The air was heavy with vivid rumours of life – the life of things infinitely small – and broken at intervals by the crackling of shots from a neighbouring shooting-range, that exploded with a sound as of champagne corks to the burden of a hollow symphony.

And then, beneath a sun which scorched the brain, and in that atmosphere charged with the ardent perfume of death, he heard a voice whispering out of the tomb where he sat. And this voice said: 'Accursed be your rifles and targets, you turbulent living ones, who care so little for the dead in their divine repose! Accursed be your ambitions and calculations, importunate mortals who study the arts of slaughter near the sanctuary of Death himself! Did you but know how easy the prize to win, how facile the end to reach, and how all save Death is naught, not so greatly would you fatigue yourselves, O ye laborious alive; nor would you so often vex the slumber of them that long ago reached the End – the only true end of life detestable!'

The Desire to Paint

(tr. Frank Pearce Sturm)

Unhappy perhaps is the man, but happy the artist, who is torn with this desire.

I burn to paint a certain woman who has appeared to me so rarely, and so swiftly fled away, like some beautiful, regrettable thing the traveller must leave behind him in the night. It is already long since I saw her.

She is beautiful, and more than beautiful: she is overpowering. The colour black preponderates in her; all that she inspires is nocturnal and profound. Her eyes are two caverns where mystery vaguely stirs and gleams; her glance illuminates like a ray of light; it is an explosion in the darkness.

I would compare her to a black sun if one could conceive of a dark star overthrowing light and happiness. But it is the moon that she makes one dream of most readily; the moon, who has without doubt touched her with her own influence; not the white moon of the idylls, who resembles a cold bride, but the sinister and intoxicating moon suspended in the depths of a stormy night, among the driven clouds; not the discreet peaceful moon who visits the dreams of pure men, but the moon torn from the sky, conquered and revolted, that the witches of Thessaly hardly constrain to dance upon the terrified grass.

Her small brow is the habitation of a tenacious will and the love of prey. And below this inquiet face, whose mobile nostrils breathe in the unknown and the impossible, glitters, with an unspeakable grace, the smile of a large mouth; white, red, and delicious; a mouth that makes one dream of the miracle of some superb flower unclosing in a volcanic land.

There are women who inspire one with the desire to woo them and win them; but she makes one wish to die slowly beneath her steady gaze.

The Glass-Vendor

(tr. Frank Pearce Sturm)

These are some natures purely contemplative and antipathetic to action, who nevertheless, under a mysterious and inexplicable impulse, sometimes act with a rapidity of which they would have believed themselves incapable. Such a one is he who, fearing to find some new vexation awaiting him at his lodgings, prowls about in a cowardly fashion before the door without daring to enter; such a one is he who keeps a letter fifteen days without opening it, or only makes up his mind at the end of six months to undertake a journey that has been a necessity for a year past. Such beings sometimes feel themselves precipitately thrust towards action, like an arrow from a bow.

The novelist and the physician, who profess to know all things, yet cannot explain whence comes this sudden and delirious energy to indolent and voluptuous souls; nor how, incapable of accomplishing the simplest and most necessary things, they are at some certain moment of time possessed by a superabundant hardihood which enables them to execute the most absurd and even the most dangerous acts.

One of my friends, the most harmless dreamer that ever lived, at one time set fire to a forest, in order to ascertain, as he said, whether the flames take hold with the easiness that is commonly affirmed. His experiment failed ten times running, on the eleventh it succeeded only too well.

Another lit a cigar by the side of a powder barrel, in

order to see, to know, to tempt Destiny, for a jest, to have the pleasure of suspense, for no reason at all, out of caprice, out of idleness. This is a kind of energy that springs from weariness and reverie; and those in whom it manifests so stubbornly are in general, as I have said, the most indolent and dreamy beings.

Another so timid that he must cast down his eyes before the gaze of any man, and summon all his poor will before he dare enter a café or pass the pay-box of a theatre, where the ticket-seller seems, in his eyes, invested with all the majesty of Minos, Æcus, and Rhadamanthus, will at times throw himself upon the neck of some old man whom he sees in the street, and embrace him with enthusiasm in sight of an astonished crowd. Why? Because – because this countenance is irresistibly attractive to him? Perhaps; but it is more legitimate to suppose that he himself does not know why.

I have been more than once a victim to these crises and outbreaks which give us cause to believe that evil-meaning demons slip into us, to make us the ignorant accomplices of their most absurd desires. One morning I arose in a sullen mood, very sad, and tired of idleness, and thrust as it seemed to me to the doing of some great thing, some brilliant act – and then, alas, I opened the window.

(I beg you to observe that in some people the spirit of mystification is not the result of labour or combination, but rather of a fortuitous inspiration which would partake, were it not for the strength of the feeling, of the mood called hysterical by the physician and satanic by those who think a little more profoundly than the physician; the mood which thrusts us unresisting to a multitude of dangerous and inconvenient acts.)

The first person I noticed in the street was a glass-vendor whose shrill and discordant cry mounted up to me through the heavy, dull atmosphere of Paris. It would have been else impossible to account for the sudden and despotic hatred of this poor man that came upon me.

'Hello, there!' I cried, and bade him ascend. Meanwhile I reflected, not without gaiety, that as my room was on the sixth landing, and the stairway very narrow, the man would have some difficulty in ascending, and in many a place would break off the corners of his fragile merchandise.

At length he appeared. I examined all his glasses with curiosity, and then said to him: 'What, have you no coloured glasses? Glasses of rose and crimson and blue, magical glasses, glasses of Paradise? You are insolent. You dare to walk in mean streets when you have no glasses that would make one see beauty in life?' And I hurried him briskly to the staircase, which he staggered down, grumbling.

I went on to the balcony and caught up a little flower-pot, and when the man appeared in the doorway beneath I let fall my engine of war perpendicularly upon the edge of his pack, so that it was upset by the shock and all his poor walking fortune broken to bits. It made a noise like a palace of crystal shattered by lightning. Mad with my folly, I cried furiously after him: 'The life beautiful! the life beautiful!'

Such nervous pleasantries are not without peril;

often enough one pays dearly for them. But what matters an eternity of damnation to him who has found in one second an eternity of enjoyment?

The Widows

(tr. Frank Pearce Sturm)

Vauvenargues says that in public gardens there are alleys haunted principally by thwarted ambition, by unfortunate inventors, by aborted glories and broken hearts, and by all those tumultuous and contracted souls in whom the last sighs of the storm mutter yet again, and who thus betake themselves far from the insolent and joyous eyes of the well-to-do. These shadowy retreats are the rendezvous of life's cripples.

To such places above all others do the poet and philosopher direct their avid conjectures. They find there an unfailing pasturage, for if there is one place they disdain to visit it is, as I have already hinted, the place of the joy of the rich. A turmoil in the void has no attractions for them. On the contrary they feel themselves irresistibly drawn towards all that is feeble, ruined, sorrowing, and bereft.

An experienced eye is never deceived. In these rigid and dejected lineaments; in these eyes, wan and hollow, or bright with the last fading gleams of the combat against fate; in these numerous profound wrinkles and in the slow and troubled gait, the eye of experience deciphers unnumbered legends of mistaken devotion, of unrewarded effort, of hunger and cold humbly and silently supported.

Have you not at times seen widows sitting on the deserted benches? Poor widows, I mean. Whether in mourning or not they are easily recognised. Moreover, there is always something wanting in the mourning of the poor; a lack of harmony which but renders it the more heart-breaking. It is forced to be niggardly in its show of grief. They are the rich who exhibit a full complement of sorrow.

Who is the saddest and most saddening of widows: she who leads by the hand a child who cannot share her reveries, or she who is quite alone? I do not know.... It happened that I once followed for several long hours an aged and afflicted woman of this kind: rigid and erect, wrapped in a little worn shawl, she carried in all her being the pride of stoicism.

She was evidently condemned by her absolute loneliness to the habits of an ancient celibacy; and the masculine characters of her habits added to their austerity a piquant mysteriousness. In what miserable café she dines I know not, nor in what manner. I followed her to a reading-room, and for a long time watched her reading the papers, her active eyes, that once burned with tears, seeking for news of a powerful and personal interest.

At length, in the afternoon, under a charming autumnal sky, one of those skies that let fall hosts of memories and regrets, she seated herself remotely in a garden, to listen, far from the crowd, to one of the regimental bands whose music gratifies the people of Paris. This was without doubt the small debauch of the innocent old woman (or the purified old woman), the well-earned consolation for another of the burdensome days without a friend, without conversation, without joy, without a confidant, that God had allowed to fall upon her perhaps for many years past – three hundred and sixty-five times a year!

Yet one more:

I can never prevent myself from throwing a glance, if not sympathetic at least full of curiosity, over the crowd of outcasts who press around the enclosure of a public concert. From the orchestra, across the night, float songs of fête, of triumph, or of pleasure. The dresses of the women sweep and shimmer; glances pass; the well-to-do, tired with doing nothing, saunter about and make indolent pretence of listening to the music. Here are only the rich, the happy; here is nothing that does not inspire or exhale the pleasure of being alive, except the aspect of the mob that presses against the outer barrier yonder, catching gratis, at the will of the wind, a tatter of music, and watching the glittering furnace within.

There is a reflection of the joy of the rich deep in the eyes of the poor that is always interesting. But to-day, beyond this people dressed in blouses and calico, I saw one whose nobility was in striking contrast with all the surrounding triviality. She was a tall, majestic woman, and so imperious in all her air that I cannot remember having seen the like in the collections of the aristocratic beauties of the past. A perfume of exalted virtue emanated from all her being. Her face, sad and worn, was in perfect keeping with the deep mourning in which she was dressed. She also, like the plebeians she mingled with and did not see, looked upon the luminous world with a profound eye, and listened with a toss of her head.

It was a strange vision. 'Most certainly,' I said to myself, 'this poverty, if poverty it be, ought not to admit of any sordid economy; so noble a face answers for that. Why then does she remain in surroundings with which she is so strikingly in contrast?'

But in curiously passing near her I was able to divine the reason. The tall widow held by the hand a child dressed like herself in black. Modest as was the price of entry, this price perhaps sufficed to pay for some of the needs of the little being, or even more, for a superfluity, a toy.

She will return on foot, dreaming and meditating – and alone, always alone, for the child is turbulent and selfish, without gentleness or patience, and cannot become, any more than another animal, a dog or a cat, the confidant of solitary griefs.

The Temptations;
Or, Eros, Plutus, and Glory

(tr. Frank Pearce Sturm)

Last night two superb Satans and a She-devil not less extraordinary ascended the mysterious stairway by which Hell gains access to the frailty of sleeping man, and communes with him in secret. These three postured gloriously before me, as though they had been upon a stage – and a sulphurous splendour emanated from these beings who so disengaged themselves from the opaque heart of the night. They bore with them so proud a presence, and so full of mastery, that at first I took them for three of the true Gods.

The first Satan, by his face, was a creature of doubtful sex. The softness of an ancient Bacchus shone in the lines of his body. His beautiful langourous eyes, of a tenebrous and indefinite colour, were like violets still laden with the heavy tears of the storm; his slightly-parted lips were like heated censers, from whence exhaled the sweet savour of many perfumes; and each time he breathed, exotic insects drew, as they fluttered, strength from the ardours of his breath.

Twined about his tunic of purple stuff, in the manner of a cincture, was an iridescent Serpent with lifted head and eyes like embers turned sleepily towards him. Phials full of sinister fluids, alternating with shining knives and instruments of surgery, hung from this living girdle. He held in his right hand a flagon containing a luminous red fluid, and inscribed with a legend in these singular words:

'DRINK OF THIS MY BLOOD: A PERFECT RESTORATIVE';

and in his left hand held a violin that without doubt served to sing his pleasures and pains, and to spread abroad the contagion of his folly upon the nights of the Sabbath.

From rings upon his delicate ankles trailed a broken chain of gold, and when the burden of this caused him to bend his eyes towards the earth, he would contemplate with vanity the nails of his feet, as brilliant and polished as well-wrought jewels.

He looked at me with eyes inconsolably heartbroken and giving forth an insidious intoxication, and cried in a chanting voice: 'If thou wilt, if thou wilt, I will make thee an overlord of souls; thou shalt be master of living matter more perfectly than the sculptor is master of his clay; thou shalt taste the pleasure, reborn without end, of obliterating thyself in the self of another, and of luring other souls to lose themselves in thine.'

But I replied to him: 'I thank thee. I only gain from this venture, then, beings of no more worth than my poor self? Though remembrance brings me shame indeed, I would forget nothing; and even before I recognised thee, thou ancient monster, thy mysterious cutlery, thy equivocal phials, and the chain that imprisons thy feet, were symbols showing clearly enough the inconvenience of thy friendship. Keep thy gifts.'

The second Satan had neither the air at once tragical and smiling, the lovely insinuating ways, nor the delicate and scented beauty of the first. A gigantic man, with a coarse, eyeless face, his heavy paunch overhung his hips and was gilded and pictured, like a tattooing, with a crowd of little moving figures which represented the unnumbered forms of universal misery. There were little sinew-shrunken men who hung themselves willingly from nails; there were meagre gnomes, deformed and under-sized, whose beseeching eyes begged an alms even more eloquently than their trembling hands; there were old mothers who nursed clinging abortions at their pendent breasts. And many others, even more surprising.

This heavy Satan beat with his fist upon his immense belly, from whence came a loud and resounding metallic clangour, which died away in a sighing made by many human voices. And he smiled unrestrainedly, showing his broken teeth – the imbecile smile of a man who has dined too freely. Then the creature said to me:

'I can give thee that which gets all, which is worth all, which takes the place of all.' And he tapped his monstrous paunch, whence came a sonorous echo as the commentary to his obscene speech. I turned away with disgust and replied: 'I need no man's misery to bring me happiness; nor will I have the sad wealth of all the misfortunes pictured upon thy skin as upon a tapestry.'

As for the She-devil, I should lie if I denied that at first I found in her a certain strange charm, which to define I can but compare to the charm of certain beautiful women past their first youth, who yet seem to age no more, whose beauty keeps something of the penetrating magic of ruins. She had an air at once imperious and sordid, and her eyes, though heavy, held a certain power of fascination. I was struck most by her voice, wherein I found the remembrance of the most delicious contralti, as well as a little of the hoarseness of a throat continually laved with brandy.

'Wouldst thou know my power?' said the charming and paradoxical voice of the false goddess. 'Then listen.' And she put to her mouth a gigantic trumpet, enribboned, like a mirliton, with the titles of all the newspapers in the world; and through this trumpet she cried my name so that it rolled through space with the sound of a hundred thousand thunders, and came re-echoing back to me from the farthest planet.

'Devil!' cried I, half tempted, 'that at least is worth something.' But it vaguely struck me, upon examining the seductive virago more attentively, that I had seen her clinking glasses with certain drolls of my acquaintance, and her blare of brass carried to my ears I know not what memory of a fanfare prostituted.

So I replied, with all disdain: 'Get thee hence! I know better than wed the light o' love of them that I will not name.'

Truly, I had the right to be proud of a so courageous renunciation. But unfortunately I awoke, and all my courage left me. 'In truth,' I said, 'I must have been very deeply asleep indeed to have had such scruples. Ah, if they would but return while I am awake, I would not be so delicate.'

So I invoked the three in a loud voice, offering to dishonour myself as often as necessary to obtain their favours; but I had without doubt too deeply offended them, for they have never returned.

The Generous Gambler

(tr. Arthur Symons)

Yesterday, across the crowd of the boulevard, I found
myself touched by a mysterious Being I had always
desired to know, and who I recognized immediately, in
spite of the fact that I had never seen him. He had, I
imagined, in himself, relatively as to me, a similar desire,
for he gave me, in passing, so significant a sign in his
eyes that I hastened to obey him. I followed him
attentively, and soon I descended behind him into a
subterranean dwelling, astonishing to me as a vision,
where shone a luxury of which none of the actual
houses in Paris could give me an approximate example.
It seemed to me singular that I had passed so often that
prodigious retreat without having discovered the
entrance. There reigned an exquisite, an almost stifling
atmosphere, which made one forget almost
instantaneously all the fastidious horrors of life; there I
breathed a sombre sensuality, like that of opium-smokers
when, set on the shore of an enchanted island, over
which shone an eternal afternoon, they felt born in
them, to the soothing sounds of melodious cascades, the
desire of never again seeing their households, their
women, their children, and of never again being tossed
on the decks of ships by storms.

There were there strange faces of men and women,
gifted with so fatal a beauty that I seemed to have seen
them years ago and in countries which I failed to
remember, and which inspired in me that curious
sympathy and that equally curious sense of fear that I

usually discover in unknown aspects. If I wanted to define in some fashion or other the singular expression of their eyes, I would say that never had I seen such magic radiance more energetically expressing the horror of ennui and of desire – of the immortal desire of feeling themselves alive.

As for mine host and myself, we were already, as we sat down, as perfect friends as if we had always known each other. We drank immeasurably of all sorts of extraordinary wines, and – a thing not less bizarre – it seemed to me, after several hours, that I was no more intoxicated than he was.

However, gambling, this superhuman pleasure, had cut, at various intervals, our copious libations, and I ought to say that I had gained and lost my soul, as we were playing, with an heroical carelessness and light-heartedness. The soul is so invisible a thing, often useless and sometimes so troublesome, that I did not experience, as to this loss, more than that kind of emotion I might have, had I lost my visiting card in the street.

We spent hours in smoking cigars, whose incomparable savour and perfume give to the soul the nostalgia of unknown delights and sights, and, intoxicated by all these spiced sauces, I dared, in an access of familiarity which did not seem to displease him, to cry, as I lifted a glass filled to the brim with wine: 'To your immortal health, Old He-Goat!'

We talked of the universe, of its creation and of its future destruction; of the leading ideas of the century—that is to say, of Progress and Perfectibility—and, in general, of all kinds of human infatuations. On this subject his Highness was inexhaustible in his irrefutable jests, and he expressed himself with a splendour of diction and with a magnificence in drollery such as I have never found in any of the most famous conversationalists of our age. He explained to me the absurdity of different philosophies that had so far taken possession of men's brains, and deigned even to take me in confidence in regard to certain fundamental principles, which I am not inclined to share with any one.

He complained in no way of the evil reputation under which he lived, indeed, all over the world, and he assured me that he himself was of all living beings the most interested in the destruction of *Superstition*, and he avowed to me that he had been afraid, relatively as to his proper power, once only, and that was on the day when he had heard a preacher, more subtle than the rest of the human herd, cry in his pulpit: 'My dear brethren, do not ever forget, when you hear the progress of lights praised, that the loveliest trick of the Devil is to persuade you that he does not exist!'

The memory of this famous orator brought us naturally on the subject of Academies, and my strange host declared to me that he didn't disdain, in many cases, to inspire the pens, the words, and the consciences of pedagogues, and that he almost always assisted in person, in spite of being invisible, at all the scientific meetings.

Encouraged by so much kindness I asked him if he had any news of God – who has not his hours of impiety? – especially as the old friend of the Devil. He said to me, with a shade of unconcern united with a deeper shade of sadness: 'We salute each other when we meet.' But, for the rest, he spoke in Hebrew.

It is uncertain if his Highness has ever given so long an audience to a simple mortal, and I feared to abuse it.

Finally, as the dark approached shivering, this famous personage, sung by so many poets, and served by so many philosophers who work for his glory's sake without being aware of it, said to me: 'I want you to remember me always, and to prove to you that I – of whom one says so much evil – am often enough *bon diable*, to make use of one of your vulgar locutions. So as to make up for the irremediable loss that you have made of your soul, I shall give you back the stake you ought to have gained, if your fate had been fortunate – that is to say, the possibility of solacing and of conquering, during your whole life, this bizarre affection of *ennui*, which is the source of all your maladies and of all your miseries. Never a desire shall be formed by you that I will not aid you to realize; you will reign over your vulgar equals; money and gold and diamonds, fairy palaces, shall come to seek you and shall ask you to accept them without your having made the least effort to obtain them; you can change your abode as often as you like; you shall have in your power all sensualities without lassitude, in lands where the climate is always hot, and where the women are as scented as the flowers.' With this he rose up and said good-bye to me with a charming smile.

If it had not been for the shame of humiliating myself before so immense an assembly, I might have voluntarily fallen at the feet of this generous Gambler, to thank him for his unheard-of munificence. But, little by little, after I had left him, an incurable defiance entered into me; I dared no longer believe in so prodigious a happiness;

and as I went to bed, making over again my nightly prayer by means of all that remained in me in the matter of faith, I repeated in my slumber: 'My God, my Lord, my God! Do let the Devil keep his word with me!'

The Eyes of the Poor

(tr. Arthur Symons)

Ah! you want to know why I hate you today. It will
probably be less easy for you to understand than for me
to explain it to you; for you are, I think, the most perfect
example of feminine impenetrability that could possibly
be found.

We had spent a long day together, and it had seemed
to me short. We had promised one another that we
would think the same thoughts and that our two souls
should become one soul; a dream which is not original,
after all, except that, dreamed by all men, it has been
realised by none.

In the evening you were a little tired, and you sat
down outside a new café at the corner of a new
boulevard, still littered with plaster and already displaying
proudly its unfinished splendours. The café glittered. The
very gas put on all the fervency of a fresh start, and
lighted up with its full force the blinding whiteness of
the walls, the dazzling sheets of glass in the mirrors, the
gilt of cornices and mouldings, the chubby-cheeked pages
straining back from hounds in leash, the ladies laughing
at the falcons on their wrists, the nymphs and goddesses
carrying fruits and pies and game on their heads, the
Hebes and Ganymedes holding out at arm's-length little
jars of syrups or parti-coloured obelisks of ices; the whole
of history and of mythology brought together to make a
paradise for gluttons. Exactly opposite to us, in the
roadway, stood a man of about forty years of age, with a
weary face and a greyish beard, holding a little boy by

one hand and carrying on the other arm a little fellow too weak to walk. He was taking the nurse-maid's place, and had brought his children out for a walk in the evening. All were in rags. The three faces were extraordinarily serious, and the six eyes stared fixedly at the new café with an equal admiration, differentiated in each according to age.

The father's eyes said: 'How beautiful it is! how beautiful it is! One would think that all the gold of the poor world had found its way to these walls.' The boy's eyes said: 'How beautiful it is! how beautiful it is! But that is a house which only people who are not like us can enter.' As for the little one's eyes, they were too fascinated to express anything but stupid and utter joy.

Song-writers say that pleasure ennobles the soul and softens the heart. The song was right that evening, so far as I was concerned. Not only was I touched by this family of eyes, but I felt rather ashamed of our glasses and decanters, so much too much for our thirst. I turned to look at you, dear love, that I might read my own thought in you; I gazed deep into your eyes, so beautiful and so strangely sweet, your green eyes that are the home of caprice and under the sovereignty of the Moon; and you said to me: 'Those people are insupportable to me with their staring saucer-eyes! Couldn't you tell the head waiter to send them away?'

So hard is it to understand one another, dearest, and so incommunicable is thought, even between people who are in love!

Windows

(tr. Arthur Symons)

He who looks in through an open window never sees so many things as he who looks at a shut window. There is nothing more profound, more mysterious, more fertile, more gloomy, or more dazzling, than a window lighted by a candle. What we can see in the sunlight is always less interesting than what goes on behind the panes of a window. In that dark or luminous hollow, life lives, life dreams, life suffers. Across the waves of roofs, I can see a woman of middle age, wrinkled, poor, who is always leaning over something, and who never goes out. Out of her face, out of her dress, out of her attitude, out of nothing almost, I have made up the woman's story, and sometimes I say it over to myself with tears.

If it had been a poor old man, I could have made up his just as easily.

And I go to bed, proud of having lived and suffered in others.

Perhaps you will say to me: 'Are you sure that it is the real story?' What does it matter, what does any reality outside of myself matter, if it has helped me to live, to feel that I am, and what I am?

Crowds

(tr. Arthur Symons)

It is not given to every man to take a bath of multitude: to play upon crowds is an art; and he alone can plunge, at the expense of humankind, into a debauch of vitality, to whom a fairy has bequeathed in his cradle the love of masks and disguises, the hate of home and the passion of travel.

Multitude, solitude: equal terms mutually convertible by the active and begetting poet. He who does not know how to people his solitude, does not know either how to be alone in a busy crowd.

The poet enjoys this incomparable privilege, to be at once himself and others. Like those wandering souls that go about seeking bodies, he enters at will the personality of every man. For him alone, every place is vacant; and if certain places seem to be closed against him, that is because in his eyes they are not worth the trouble of visiting.

The solitary and thoughtful walker derives a singular intoxication from this universal communion. He who mates easily with the crowd knows feverish joys that must be for ever unknown to the egoist, shut up like a coffer, and to the sluggard, imprisoned like a shell-fish. He adopts for his own all the occupations, all the joys and all the sorrows that circumstance sets before him.

What men call love is small indeed, narrow and weak indeed, compared with this ineffable orgie, this sacred prostitution of the soul which gives itself up wholly (poetry and charity!) to the unexpected which happens, to the stranger as he passes.

It is good sometimes that the happy of this world should learn, were it only to humble their foolish pride for an instant, that there are higher, wider, and rarer joys than theirs. The founders of colonies, the shepherds of nations, the missionary priests, exiled to the ends of the earth, doubtless know something of these mysterious intoxications; and, in the midst of the vast family that their genius has raised about them, they must sometimes laugh at the thought of those who pity them for their chaste lives and troubled fortunes.

The Cake

(tr. Arthur Symons)

I was travelling. The landscape in the midst of which I
was seated was of an irresistible grandeur and sublimity.
Something no doubt at that moment passed from it into
my soul. My thoughts fluttered with a lightness like that
of the atmosphere; vulgar passions, such as hate and
profane love, seemed to me now as far away as the clouds
that floated in the gulfs beneath my feet; my soul seemed
to me as vast and pure as the dome of the sky that
enveloped me; the remembrance of earthly things came as
faintly to my heart as the thin tinkle or the bells of
unseen herds, browsing far, far away, on the slope of
another mountain. Across the little motionless lake, black
with the darkness of its immense depth, there passed
from time to time the shadow of a cloud, like the shadow
of an airy giant's cloak, flying through heaven. And I
remember that this rare and solemn sensation, caused by
a vast and perfectly silent movement, filled me with
mingled joy and fear. In a word, thanks to the enrapturing
beauty about me, I felt that I was at perfect peace with
myself and with the universe; I even believe that, in my
complete forgetfulness of all earthly evil, I had come to
think the newspapers are right after all, and man was born
good; when, incorrigible matter renewing its exigences, I
sought to refresh the fatigue and satisfy the appetite caused
by so lengthy a climb. I took from my pocket a large piece
of bread, a leathern cup, and a small bottle of a certain
elixir which the chemists at that time sold to tourists, to be
mixed, on occasion, with liquid snow.

I was quietly cutting my bread when a slight noise made me look up. I saw in front of me a little ragged urchin, dark and dishevelled, whose hollow eyes, wild and supplicating, devoured the piece of bread. And I heard him gasp, in a low, hoarse voice, the word: 'Cake!' I could not help laughing at the appellation with which he thought fit to honour my nearly white bread, and I cut off a big slice and offered it to him. Slowly he came up to me, not taking his eyes from the coveted object; then, snatching it out of my hand, he stepped quickly back, as if he feared that my offer was not sincere, or that I had already repented of it.

But at the same instant he was knocked over by another little savage, who had sprung from I know not where, and who was so precisely like the first that one might have taken them for twin brothers. They rolled over on the ground together, struggling for the possession of the precious booty, neither willing to share it with his brother. The first, exasperated, clutched the second by the hair; and the second seized one of the ears of the first between his teeth, and spat out a little bleeding morsel with a fine oath in dialect. The legitimate proprietor of the cake tried to hook his little claws into the usurper's eyes; the latter did his best to throttle his adversary with one hand, while with the other he endeavoured to slip the prize of war into his pocket. But, heartened by despair, the loser pulled himself together, and sent the victor sprawling with a blow of the head in his stomach. Why describe a hideous fight which indeed lasted longer than their childish strength seemed to promise? The cake travelled from hand to hand, and changed from pocket to pocket, at every moment; but, alas, it changed also in size;

and when at length, exhausted, panting and bleeding, they stopped from the sheer impossibility of going on, there was no longer any cause of feud; the slice of bread had disappeared, and lay scattered in crumbs like the grains of sand with which it was mingled.

The sight had darkened the landscape for me, and dispelled the joyous calm in which my soul had lain basking; I remained saddened for quite a long time, saying over and over to myself: 'There is then a wonderful country in which bread is called cake, and is so rare a delicacy that it is enough in itself to give rise to a war literally fratricidal!'

Evening Twilight

(tr. Arthur Symons)

The day is over. A great restfulness descends into poor minds that the day's work has wearied; and thoughts take on the tender and dim colours of twilight.

Nevertheless from the mountain peak there comes to my balcony, through the transparent clouds of evening, a great clamour, made up of a crowd of discordant cries, dulled by distance into a mournful harmony, like that of the rising tide or of a storm brewing.

Who are the hapless ones to whom evening brings no calm; to whom, as to the owls, the coming of night is the signal for a witches' sabbath? The sinister ululation comes to me from the hospital on the mountain; and, in the evening, as I smoke, and look down on the quiet of the immense valley, bristling with houses, each of whose windows seems to say, 'Here is peace, here is domestic happiness!' I can, when the wind blows from the heights, lull my astonished thought with this imitation of the harmonies of hell.

Twilight excites madmen. I remember I had two friends whom twilight made quite ill. One of them lost all sense of social and friendly amenities, and flew at the first-comer like a savage. I have seen him throw at the waiter's head an excellent chicken, in which he imagined he had discovered some insulting hieroglyph. Evening, harbinger of profound delights, spoilt for him the most succulent things.

The other, a prey to disappointed ambition, turned gradually, as the daylight dwindled, sourer, more gloomy, more nettlesome. Indulgent and sociable during the day, he was pitiless in the evening; and it was not only on others, but on himself, that he vented the rage of his twilight mania.

The former died mad, unable to recognise his wife and child; the latter still keeps the restlessness of a perpetual disquietude; and, if all the honours that republics and princes can confer were heaped upon him, I believe that the twilight would still quicken in him the burning envy of imaginary distinctions. Night, which put its own darkness into their minds, brings light to mine; and, though it is by no means rare for the same cause to bring about opposite results, I am always as it were perplexed and alarmed by it.

O night! O refreshing dark! for me you are the summons to an inner feast, you are the deliverer from anguish! In the solitude of the plains, in the stony labyrinths of a city, scintillation of stars, outburst of gaslamps, you are the fireworks of the goddess Liberty!

Twilight, how gentle you are and how tender! The rosy lights that still linger on the horizon, like the last agony of day under the conquering might of its night; the flaring candle flames that stain with dull red the last glories of the sunset; the heavy draperies that an invisible hand draws out of the depths of the East, mimic all those complex feelings that war on one another in the heart of man at the solemn moments of life.

Would you not say that it was one of those strange costumes worn by dancers, in which the tempered splendours of a shining skirt show through a dark and transparent gauze, as, through the darkness of the present, pierces the delicious past? And the wavering stars of gold

and silver with which it is shot, are they not those fires
of fancy which take light never so well as under the deep
mourning of the night?

'Anywhere out of the World'

(tr. Arthur Symons)

Life is a hospital, in which every patient is possessed by the desire of changing his bed. One would prefer to suffer near the fire, and another is certain that he would get well if he were by the window. It seems to me that I should always be happy if I were somewhere else, and this question of moving house is one that I am continually talking over with my soul.

'Tell me, my soul, poor chilly soul, what do you say to living in Lisbon? It must be very warm there, and you would bask merrily, like a lizard. It is by the sea; they say that it is built of marble, and that the people have such a horror of vegetation that they tear up all the trees. There is a country after your own soul; a country made up of light and mineral, and with liquid to reflect them.'

My soul makes no answer.

'Since you love rest, and to see moving things, will you come and live in that heavenly land, Holland? Perhaps you would be happy in a country which you have so often admired in pictures. What do you say to Rotterdam, you who love forests of masts, and ships anchored at the doors of houses?'

My soul remains silent.

'Or perhaps Java seems to you more attractive? Well, there we shall find the mind of Europe married to tropical beauty.'

Not a word. Can my soul be dead?

'Have you sunk then into so deep a stupor that only your own pain gives you pleasure? If that be so, let us go to the lands that are made in the likeness of Death. I know exactly the place for us, poor soul! We will book our passage to Torneo. We will go still further, to the last limits of the Baltic; and, if it be possible, further still from life; we will make our abode at the Pole. There the sun only grazes the earth, and the slow alternations of light and night put out variety and bring in the half of nothingness, monotony. There we can take great baths of darkness, while, from time to time, for our pleasure, the Aurora Borealis shall scatter its rosy sheaves before us, like reflections of fireworks in hell!'

At last my soul bursts into speech, and wisely she cries to me: 'Anywhere, anywhere, out of the world!'

A Heroic Death

(tr. Arthur Symons)

Fancioulle was an admirable buffoon, and almost one of
the friends of the Prince. But for persons professionally
devoted to the comic, serious things have a fatal
attraction, and, strange as it may seem that ideas of
patriotism and liberty should seize despotically upon the
brain of a player, one day Fancioulle joined in a
conspiracy formed by some, discontented nobles.

There exist everywhere sensible men to denounce
those individuals of atrabiliar disposition who seek to
depose princes, and, without consulting it, to reconstitute
society. The lords in question were arrested, together with
Fancioulle, and condemned to death.

I would readily believe that the Prince was almost sorry
to find his favourite actor among the rebels. The Prince
was neither better nor worse than any other prince; but an
excessive sensibility rendered him, in many cases, more
cruel and more despotic than all his fellows. Passionately
enamoured of the fine arts, an excellent connoisseur as
well, he was truly insatiable of pleasures. Indifferent
enough in regard to men and morals, himself a real artist,
he feared no enemy but Ennui, and the extravagant efforts
that he made to fly or to vanquish this tyrant of the world
would certainly have brought upon him, on the part of a
severe historian, the epithet of 'monster,' had it been
permitted, in his dominions, to write anything whatever
which did not tend exclusively to pleasure, or to
astonishment, which is one of the most delicate forms of
pleasure. The great misfortune of the Prince was that he

had no theatre vast enough for his genius. There are young Neros who are stifled within too narrow limits, and whose names and whose intentions will never be known to future ages. An unforeseeing Providence had given to this man faculties greater than his dominions.

Suddenly the rumour spread that the sovereign had decided to pardon all the conspirators; and the origin of this rumour was the announcement of a special performance in which Fancioulle would play one of his best roles, and at which even the condemned nobles, it was said, were to be present, an evident sign, added superficial minds, of the generous tendencies of the Prince.

On the part to a man so naturally and deliberately eccentric, anything was possible, even virtue, even mercy, especially if he could hope to find in it unexpected pleasures. But to those who, like myself, had succeeded in penetrating further into the depths of this sick and curious soul, it was infinitely more probable that the Prince was wishful to estimate the quality of the scenic talents of a man condemned to death. He would profit by the occasion to obtain a physiological experience of a capital interest, and to verify to what extent the habitual faculties of an artist would be altered or modified by the extraordinary situation in which he found himself. Beyond this, did there exist in his mind an intention, more or less defined, of mercy? It is a point that has never been solved.

At last, the great day having come, the little court displayed all its pomps, and it would be difficult to realise, without having seen it, what splendour the privileged classes of a little state with limited resources can show forth, on a really solemn occasion. This was a doubly solemn one, both from the wonder of its display and from the mysterious moral interest attaching to it.

The Sieur Fancioulle excelled especially in parts either silent or little burdened with words, such as are often the principal ones in those fairy plays whose object is to represent symbolically the mystery of life. He came upon the stage lightly and with a perfect ease, which in itself lent some support, in the minds of the noble public, to the idea of kindness and forgiveness.

When we say of an actor, 'This is a good actor,' we make use of a formula which implies that under the personage we can still distinguish the actor, that is to say, art, effort, will. Now, if an actor should succeed in being, in relation to the personage whom he is appointed to express, precisely what the finest statues of antiquity, miraculously animated, living, walking, seeing, would be in relation to the confused general idea of beauty, this would be, undoubtedly, a singular and unheard of case. Fancioulle was, that evening, a perfect idealisation, which it was impossible not to suppose living, possible, real. The buffoon came and went, he laughed, wept, was convulsed, with an indestructible aureole about his head, an aureole invisible to all, but visible to me, and in which were blended, in a strange amalgam, the rays of Art and the martyr's glory. Fancioulle brought, by I know not what special grace, something divine and supernatural into even the most extravagant buffooneries. My pen trembles, and the tears of an emotion which I cannot forget rise to my eyes, as I try to describe to you this never-to-be-forgotten evening. Fancioulle proved to me, in a peremptory, an irrefutable way, that the intoxication of Art is surer than all others to veil the terrors of the gulf;

that genius can act a comedy on the threshold of the grave with a joy that hinders it from seeing the grave, lost, as it is, in a Paradise shutting out all thought of the grave and of destruction.

The whole audience, *blasé* and frivolous as it was, soon fell under the all-powerful sway of the artist. Not a thought was left of death, of mourning, or of punishment. All gave themselves up, without disquietude, to the manifold delights caused by the sight of a masterpiece of living art. Explosions of joy and admiration again and again shook the dome of the edifice with the energy of a continuous thunder. The Prince himself, in an ecstasy, joined in the applause of his court.

Nevertheless, to a discerning eye, his emotion was not unmixed. Did he feel himself conquered in his power as despot? humiliated in his art as the striker of terror into hearts, of chill into souls? Such suppositions, not exactly justified, but not absolutely unjustifiable, passed through my mind as I contemplated the face of the Prince, on which a new pallor gradually overspread its habitual paleness, as snow overspreads snow. His lips compressed themselves tighter and tighter, and his eyes lighted up with an inner fire like that of jealousy or of spite, even while he applauded the talents of his old friend, the strange buffoon, who played the buffoon so well in the face of death. At a certain moment, I saw his Highness lean towards a little page, stationed behind him, and whisper in his ear. The roguish face of the pretty child lit up with a smile, and he briskly quitted the Prince's box as if to execute some urgent commission.

A few minutes later a shrill and prolonged hiss interrupted Fancioulle in one of his finest moments, and rent alike every ear and heart. And from the part of the house from whence this unexpected note of disapproval had sounded, a child darted into a corridor with stifled laughter.

Fancioulle, shaken, roused out of his dream, closed his eyes, then re-opened them, almost at once, extraordinarily wide, opened his mouth as if to breathe convulsively, staggered a little forward, a little backward, and then fell stark dead on the boards.

Had the hiss, swift as a sword, really frustrated the hangman? Had the Prince himself divined all the homicidal efficacy of his ruse? It is permitted to doubt it. Did he regret his dear and inimitable Fancioulle? It is sweet and legitimate to believe it.

The guilty nobles had enjoyed the performance of comedy for the last time They were effaced from life.

Since then, many mimes, justly appreciated in different countries, have played before the court of —; but none of them have ever been able to recall the marvellous talents of Fancioulle, or to rise to the same favour.

Epilogue

(tr. Arthur Symons)

With heart at rest I climbed the citadel's
Steep height, and saw the city as from a tower,
Hospital, brothel, prison, and such hells,

Where evil comes up softly like a flower.
Thou knowest, O Satan, patron of my pain,
Not for vain tears I went up at that hour;

But, like an old sad faithful lecher, fain
To drink delight of that enormous trull
Whose hellish beauty makes me young again.

Whether thou sleep, with heavy vapours full,
Sodden with day, or, new apparelled, stand
In gold-laced veils of evening beautiful,

I love thee, infamous city! Harlots and
Hunted have pleasures of their own to give,
The vulgar herd can never understand.

INDEX OF FIRST LINES

Poems